Social Issues
in Literature

Peer Pressure
in Robert Cormier's
The Chocolate War

Other Books in the Social Issues in Literature Series:

Social Issues
in Literature

Peer Pressure
in Robert Cormier's
The Chocolate War

Dedria Bryfonski, Book Editor

GREENHAVEN PRESS
A part of Gale, Cengage Learning

GALE
CENGAGE Learning™

Detroit • New York • San Francisco • New Haven, Conn • Waterville, Maine • London

Christine Nasso, *Publisher*
Elizabeth Des Chenes, *Managing Editor*

© 2010 Greenhaven Press, a part of Gale, Cengage Learning

Gale and Greenhaven Press are registered trademarks used herein under license.

For more information, contact:
Greenhaven Press
27500 Drake Rd.
Farmington Hills, MI 48331-3535
Or you can visit our Internet site at gale.cengage.com

For product information and technology assistance, contact us at

Gale Customer Support, 1-800-877-4253
For permission to use material from this text or product, submit all requests online at www.cengage.com/permissions

Further permissions questions can be emailed to permissionrequest@cengage.com

Articles in Greenhaven Press anthologies are often edited for length to meet page requirements. In addition, original titles of these works are changed to clearly present the main thesis and to explicitly indicate the author's opinion. Every effort is made to ensure that Greenhaven Press accurately reflects the original intent of the authors. Every effort has been made to trace the owners of copyrighted material.

Cover image by Margaret Bourke-White/Time & Life Pictures/Getty Images.

LIBRARY OF CONGRESS CATALOGING-IN-PUBLICATION DATA

Peer pressure in Robert Cormier's The chocolate war / Dedria Bryfonski, book editor.
　　　p. cm. -- (Social issues in literature)
　　Includes bibliographical references and index.
　　ISBN 978-0-7377-4620-4
　　ISBN 978-0-7377-4621-1 (pbk.)
　　1. Cormier, Robert. Chocolate war. 2. Peer pressure in adolescence--Juvenile literature. 3. Teenagers in literature. I. Bryfonski, Dedria.
　　PS3553.O653C477 2009
　　813'.54--dc22
　　　　　　　　　　　　　　　　　　　　　　　　　　　　　　　　　2009018275

Printed in the United States of America
1 2 3 4 5 6 7 13 12 11 10 09

Contents

Chapter 1: Background on Robert Cormier

Chapter 2: *The Chocolate War* and Peer Pressure

Chapter 3: Contemporary Perspectives on Peer Pressure

Introduction

Robert Cormier was one of the most controversial and highly acclaimed authors of young-adult novels. His books address serious topics—including bullying, terrorism, death, incest, rape—and rarely have happy endings. While some reviewers have criticized Cormier's novels as bleak and pessimistic, young readers are drawn to his combination of realism and sensitivity. As Cormier said in an interview with *Authors and Artists for Young Adults*, "A lot of people underestimate that intelligent teenager out there. These kids today, I'm talking about the sensitive, intelligent kid, are really far ahead of a lot of adults. They have been exposed to so much. Anybody who writes down to these people is making a mistake."

Cormier was born in the French Canadian sector of Leominster, Massachusetts, and he spent most of his life in the surrounding area. After attending Fitchburg State College, he began a career as a journalist in 1946, first with radio station WTAG, then with the *Worcester Telegraph & Gazette*, and finally with the *Fitchburg Sentinel and Enterprise*. For many years, Cormier blended his career as a journalist with creative writing. He wrote three adult novels in the 1960s. The first, *Now and at the Hour*, was inspired by his father's death from cancer. His next two books, *A Little Raw on Monday Mornings* and *Take Me Where the Good Times Are*, were both drawn from people Cormier had interviewed as a journalist. All three books were only moderately successful. His first young-adult novel, *The Chocolate War*, was published in 1974. It was followed by *I Am the Cheese* in 1977. The success of these two young-adult novels enabled Cormier to resign his position at the newspaper and devote himself full-time to writing fiction.

It has been widely reported that an event in Cormier's life inspired *The Chocolate War*. His son was a freshman in high school and came home one day with a bag of chocolates that he was supposed to sell for a school fund-raiser, but did not want to. Cormier supported his son in that decision, but he wondered what might have happened to his son in different circumstances, and such wondering led to the conception of *The Chocolate War*. What is less well known is that Cormier himself was the target of bullying in high school, a topic he addressed in a human-interest column that he wrote periodically for the *Fitchburg Sentinel and Enterprise* titled And So On. The following is an excerpt from that column, which was titled "Meet the Bully":

> He used to wait for me after school, not every day, of course, but often enough so that he became a regular and sinister presence in my life. And he seldom waited in the same place. Sometimes he'd be lurking on a street that I took as a short-cut home. Other times he'd station himself near the drug-store where I stopped occasionally—when I had the money—to buy those six-for-a-penny butterscotch candies or take swift glances at the latest Action Comics, which featured Superman.
>
> Anyway, there he'd be—my enemy, my nemesis: the bully.
>
> He was older than I was and bigger—bullies often are. He was about fifteen or sixteen and I was about twelve or thirteen. He seemed to be going bald, even at that age. At least, his hair was thinning and you could see his white skull and this made him seem more sinister somehow.
>
> But I could run faster than he could. That was my saving grace. I would encounter him on the street and he'd be waiting for me. We never spoke a word—but he looked at me with such a glitter of triumph and with such malice that instinctively I would head the other way. Sometimes he wouldn't challenge me but merely watch me change my course. Other times he chased me. And off I'd go.

It is intriguing to note that this column about Cormier's memory of high school bullying was published on April 11, 1974, the same year he was writing *The Chocolate War*.

In choosing bullying and peer pressure as themes for his first young-adult novel, Cormier found a subject that resonated with a young-adult audience. School bullying has become increasingly prevalent in the United States, with approximately 30 percent of teens estimated to be involved in bullying either as a perpetrator or a victim. Bullying is more common in younger teens than in older teens, and more common among boys than girls. In a recent national study of students in grades six through ten, 13 percent admitted bullying others, 11 percent said they were the victims of bullying, and 6 percent were both victims and perpetrators of bullying.

What is surprising to some about these statistics is the number of teens who, having been on the receiving end of bullying, also become bullies themselves. This is not the path chosen by Jerry in *The Chocolate War*. Jerry goes against peer pressure and decides not to sell chocolate for his school, thus disrupting the power structure of the school. He is punished for this infraction by the school bullies—psychologically by Archie Costello and physically by Emile Janza.

At the conclusion of *The Chocolate War*, Jerry is defeated, discouraged, and devastatingly injured. Some critics, however, have asserted that, in a larger sense, Jerry is victorious because he made a moral choice, held fast to his convictions, and maintained his humanity. The viewpoints that follow examine peer pressure, and particularly bullying, in *The Chocolate War*, exploring many facets of the novel. Critics offer divergent views about whether Cormier presents an outlook that is bleak and desolate or realistic but hopeful. In addition, several viewpoints address peer pressure, conformity, and bullying in twenty-first-century America, examining causes and possible methods of prevention.

Chronology

1925

Robert Edmund Cormier is born in Leominister, Massachusetts, on January 17 to Lucien Joseph Cormier, a French Canadian, and Irma Margaret Collins Cormier, an Irish American, the second of their eight children.

1943–1944

Cormier works the night shift at the Leominister comb factory so that he can attend Fitchburg State College during the day. His short story "The Little Things That Count" is published in *Sign*.

1944

Cormier drops out of college and begins writing commercials for radio station WTAG in Worcester, Massachusetts.

1948

Cormier and Constance Senay are married on November 6. Cormier begins working as a night bureau man for the *Worcester Telegram & Gazette*.

1955

Cormier begins working days as a reporter and wire editor for the *Fitchburg Sentinel*. He works for the *Sentinel* until 1978, as a reporter, book review editor, wire editor, associate editor, and associate city editor.

1960

Now and at the Hour is published.

1963

A Little Raw on Monday Mornings is published.

1965

Take Me Where the Good Times Are is published.

1974

The Chocolate War is published.

1977

I Am the Cheese is published.

1979

After the First Death is published.

1980

Eight Plus One is published.

1983

The Bumblebee Flies Anyway is published.

1985

Beyond the Chocolate War is published.

1988

Fade is published.

1990

Other Bells for Us to Ring is published.

1991

We All Fall Down is published. Cormier receives the Margaret A. Edwards Award for *The Chocolate War, I Am the Cheese,* and *After the First Death.*

1992

Tunes for Bears to Dance To is published.

1995

In the Middle of the Night is published.

1997

Tenderness is published.

1998

Heroes is published.

1999

Frenchtown Summer is published.

2000

Cormier dies on November 2 in Boston.

2001

The Rag and Bone Shop is published posthumously.

CHAPTER 1

Background on
Robert Cormier

The Life of Robert Cormier

Sylvia Patterson Iskander

Sylvia Patterson Iskander is professor emerita of literature at the University of Louisiana–Lafayette.

Sylvia Patterson Iskander finds Robert Cormier unique among writers of young-adult fiction because of his controversial subject matter, suspenseful plots, and uncompromising realism. Cormier's novels, she explains, explore themes of evil, power, guilt, corruption, and complacency. His subjects are profound—death, terrorism, violence, and gangs—and he confronts them with a bleak honesty.

"Teen-agers' Laureate," the title conferred upon Robert Cormier by Tony Schwartz in *Newsweek*, is fittingly bestowed upon this widely read and critically acclaimed author in the somewhat amorphous genre referred to as young-adult literature. For many years a journalist, newspaper editor, and author of fiction, Robert Cormier never wrote for a young-adult audience until first his agent, then his publisher, suggested that *The Chocolate War* (1974) would be a fine young-adult book. Although Cormier did not change any aspect of his writing—perhaps a key to his success—he became known as a young-adult writer. Treating subjects such as terrorism, fear, power, betrayal, death, and courage, Cormier creates unforgettable stories that are suspenseful, psychologically thrilling, and bleak in outlook. Although Cormier's subject matter and pessimism sometimes give rise to controversy, there is no controversy about the clarity of his style, with its vivid figures of speech, lack of sentimentality, and refusal to patronize, or the wholehearted acceptance of his novels by teenagers.

Sylvia Patterson Iskander, "Robert Cormier," in *Concise Dictionary of Literary Biography: Broadening Views, 1968–1988*, Detroit: Gale Research Co., 1989, pp. 34–51. Reproduced by permission of Gale, a part of Cengage Learning.

The question arising most often among adult readers is: What kind of person could write such harshly realistic and pessimistic books for young people? Young adults appear to understand Cormier better; they are able to perceive that his novels are not entirely without hope. They ask other types of questions, offer praise, and accept the inevitable conclusions of the stories. Uncompromising in his pursuit of truth, Cormier has explained that he sees his novels as an antidote to the artificial realism of television, where one is always aware that the hero will survive to appear next week. . . .

A Writer in My Soul

Born in the French Hill section of Leominster, Massachusetts, on 17 January 1925, Robert Edmund Cormier was one of eight children. When he was five, however, his three-year-old brother died. His father, Lucien Joseph Cormier, whose family was originally from Quebec, had moved to Leominster in 1910. Lucien Cormier, like many other French-Canadian Catholic settlers in the area, supported his family by working in factories in or near Leominster, a typical New England town about fifty miles west of Boston. Cormier's mother, Irma Margaret Collins, who was Irish, created a home that the author describes as "warm, happy, and loving." In his short stories and in his early novels, which often include autobiographical elements, he frequently depicts caring, dedicated family members.

In a personal interview at the Cormier home on 3 July 1980, Cormier recalled his adolescent years outside the home in quite a different fashion. He described himself as an introvert who felt like an outsider in school. His ambition to become an author apparently stemmed from the pronouncement of his seventh-grade teacher, Sister Catherine, who told him that he was a writer after reading a poem he had written. Cormier revealed to William A. Davis that he considered himself thereafter "a writer in my soul." This conviction enabled him to become more extroverted in high school when he began to write for the yearbook, to act in plays, and to sing in the chorus. In the ninth grade he read Thomas Wolfe's *The Web and the Rock*. Wolfe's story of a young boy living in a small town, hungry for love and fame, struck a responsive chord in Cormier.

After his graduation from high school in 1942, Cormier took a job in a Leominster comb factory, working the night shift so that he could attend Fitchburg State College during the day. There he met Professor Florence Conlon, who encouraged him to write a short story. "The Little Things That Count," a story about an American soldier wounded in World War II, was the result. Professor Conlon submitted Cormier's story to *Sign*, a Catholic magazine, which accepted it and paid seventy-five dollars to the elated nineteen-year-old writer. Meanwhile, Cormier realized that the education he was receiving at Fitchburg State College, which was designed to educate primary-school teachers, was not what he wanted, so he dropped out. Years later, in 1977, Fitchburg State College conferred upon him an honorary Doctor of Letters degree. In 1981 Cormier presented his manuscripts to the college for a permanent collection.

Shortly after leaving college, Cormier accepted a series of writing jobs. The first, in 1946, was writing commercials for radio station WTAG in Worcester, Massachusetts. No doubt the discipline of compressing ideas and information into a hundred words or fewer contributed to Cormier's terse, fast-paced style of writing. Those stylistic elements are traceable as well to the influence of Ernest Hemingway and William Saroyan, both writers whom Cormier greatly admires.

In 1948, Cormier married Constance Senay and began working as a night bureau man for the *Worcester Telegram and Gazette*. After five years there he accepted an offer from the *Fitchburg Sentinel* to work days. His job required him to cover all aspects of small-town life. A good reporter and wire editor, Cormier excelled when it came to human interest stories.

Journalist by Day, Fiction Writer by Night

The Associated Press Award for Best News Story in New England in 1959 went to Cormier for his story about a child severely burned in an automobile accident. The story resulted in a fund being established to help defray the child's medical expenses. In 1973 Cormier was again the recipient of the Associated Press Award, this time for a story written from the perspective of mentally retarded people. The next year, Cormier received still another award for journalism; K.R. Thomson Newspapers, Inc., an international chain, honored the writer for a human interest column written for the *Fitchburg Sentinel* under the pseudonym of John Fitch IV.

While Cormier worked days for the newspaper, he wrote fiction on weekends and at night. Many of his stories were accepted by magazines such as *Redbook, Saturday Evening Post, Woman's Day,* and *McCall's,* and some of these were later collected in *Eight Plus One.* He also wrote three novels for adults, which were published between 1960 and 1965. At the same time he did some public relations writing to help support his growing family. He was associate editor of the *Fitchburg-Leominster Sentinel and Enterprise* when he resigned on 14 January 1978 to devote all his time to writing fiction.

Most of Cormier's works are set in the fictitious town of Monument, Massachusetts, a composite of Leominster and Fitchburg. The models or prototypes for many scenes from Cormier's works can be found in or near these two typical New England towns. The Cormier family has lived in a two-storied, shingled house midway between them for some forty years.

Cormier works every morning in a book-lined alcove off his dining room, where he says most of his ideas come to him. He thinks in terms of what is going to happen to a certain character that day, not in terms of writing so many words or pages a day, and he thinks in terms of scenes, not segments or chapters. A superb craftsman and stylist, Cormier rewrites continuously, sharpening phrases and metaphors and deleting passages that do not advance the plot. He usually does not know the entire plot in advance. A great lover of mystery stories and suspense novels, an admirer of Graham Greene, John le Carré, Ellery Queen, and Ed McBain, Cormier recognizes the reader's desire for straightforward action, not lengthy description. Thus he uses vivid similes and metaphors that evoke images or emotions without long descriptive passages, a writing technique compatible with the taste of young people geared to the action-packed age of television.

This style is evident even in Cormier's first novel, *Now and at the Hour* (1960), written for adults and inspired by Cormier's grief over the death of his father, whom he admired and loved. Cormier describes himself as an emotional writer who seeks to arouse emotion in his readers and relies upon his own emotional involvement to complete a work. *Now and at the Hour*, a work in which Cormier's emotional involvement is still strong after so many years, effectively transmits his feelings to the reader. . . .

Two more adult novels followed *Now and at the Hour: A Little Raw on Monday Mornings* (1963), the story of thirty-eight-year-old Gracie, a widowed Catholic factory worker who finds herself pregnant and considers abortion; and *Take Me Where the Good Times Are* (1965), the story of seventy-year-old Tommy Bartin, resident of a poorhouse. Tommy is one of those characters most difficult to portray convincingly: a good man.

First Young-Adult Novel

Cormier's fourth novel, however, changed his life and his audience. His agent read the first forty pages of *The Chocolate War* (1974) and told him that he had a young-adult novel.

Cormier worried about bad language and sex scenes, but his agent recommended that he write as he ordinarily did. He followed this advice, refusing to change the downbeat ending, which caused several publishers to reject the book before it was accepted by Pantheon.

The story of Jerry Renault's courageous stand against peer pressure and against the corrupt headmaster of his high school is not pessimistic, but the fact that Jerry stands alone and is physically and mentally beaten at the close of the novel seems to break an unstated requirement of young-adult fiction that there must be some hope, something positive for teenagers to assimilate. No doubt Jerry's parting advice to his friend Goober—to go with the crowd and not to "dare disturb the universe"—is grimly pessimistic, yet most of the novel depicts courage and bravery in the face of overwhelming odds. Jerry does not win, but his fight provides an inspiration or a warning that more people need to take a stand, to support what they believe in, to "dare disturb the universe." . . .

Cormier seems especially talented at recognizing everyday events as possible topics for his fiction. He has revealed that the impetus for *The Chocolate War* was an incident involving his son, Peter, who came home one day with a bag of chocolates to sell for his high school. Peter did not want to sell them, and Cormier supported his decision; however, the next day as he watched Peter walk up to the door of the school with the unsold candy, he wondered what he had done to his son. Luckily there were no repercussions for Peter; instead, the incident set off a spark in Cormier's imagination: What if there had been opposition?. . .

Some critics have compared *The Chocolate War* to J.D. Salinger's *The Catcher in the Rye* or William Golding's *Lord of the Flies*. Despite its controversial subject matter, its literary qualities are indisputable. Included in the American Library Association's Best Books for Young Adults for 1974, and in their Best of the Best for 1970–1982, it was also a *New York*

Times Notable Book for the Year. It was awarded starred reviews in *Kirkus* and *School Library Journal,* and it received the Maxi Award. Foreign editions have been published in England, Italy, France, Germany, Spain, Denmark, Holland, and Sweden. In 1988, *The Chocolate War* was made into a movie, now available on videocassette [and DVD], which follows the spirit of the novel closely in the early and middle scenes but drastically changes the ending.

Novels Challenge Complacency

Cormier's second young-adult novel is also powerful and provocative. The full impact of *I Am the Cheese* (1977) does not hit the reader until the final pages as two seemingly separate stories merge, and the reader perceives the illusory nature of reality presented here. Adam Farmer, the fourteen-year-old protagonist, is a sensitive youth who recognizes that there are some strange happenings in his home: his mother calls someone every Thursday evening; his father has periodic visits by the mysterious Mr. Grey; Adam even discovers two birth certificates in his name, each with a different birthdate. Thus problems of identity are obviously central to this novel. Adam learns that his real name is Paul Delmonte and that his mother calls her sister once a week (Adam had thought that he had no living relatives). His father tells him that Mr. Grey is with the Department of Re-identification and that the Delmontes had to take on a new identity because Mr. Delmonte had testified on behalf of the government about connections between organized crime and certain government agencies. . . .

The powerlessness of the individual to stand alone against a corrupt society is another theme of this emotionally riveting novel. Cormier goes a step beyond *The Chocolate War,* for here Anthony Delmonte, an adult, is able to withstand the destructive forces moving against him only for a period of ten years or so. How then is it possible for a fourteen-year-old boy to succeed in standing alone against overwhelming corruption and evil? Yet Adam is brave, and his instincts are valid; he senses the evil in Brint [a psychiatrist or government spy] but can do nothing, for he is kept drugged in an institution and allowed to return to reality only once a year, on the anniversary of the death of his parents. His failure to recall what happened to his family is the only reason that he is allowed to live. If he ever does remember, he will be "terminated." . . .

Indeed, the novel is bleak, but it is also thought-provoking. *I Am the Cheese* questions long-held assumptions about the nature of patriotism and governmental agencies and about truth and identity. . . .

Another carefully structured novel, *After the First Death* (1979), also shatters the reader's complacency. It interweaves the story of three teenagers. First is Ben Marchand, a general's son, a sensitive young student at Castleton Academy, who longs to know and understand his father but ultimately cannot live with the knowledge that his father's patriotism is more important to him than is Ben himself. Second is Miro Shantas, a refugee, orphaned at an early age and trained as a terrorist. He is scheduled to go on his first assignment, to kill for the first time; his target is the driver of a hijacked busload of first graders. And third is Kate Forrester, a beautiful eighteen-year-old blonde who, as the substitute bus driver the day of the hijacking, learns much about herself.

After the First Death opens at Castleton, where Ben is writing about his life, about the bullet wound in his chest. The time is two weeks before Christmas, but there are flashbacks to the preceding August when four terrorists hijacked the busload of sixteen children. Ben acts as a go-between for Inner Delta—the special secret agency stationed at Fort Delta, a local army base—and the hijackers, whose unnamed homeland is perhaps in the Middle East. The book alternates between chapters involving Ben and his father and chapters involving the hijacking. Though the novel is twelve chapters long, the climactic meeting of Ben and the terrorists does not occur until chapter 10. In what has become typical Cormier form, chapters 11 and 12 are not just dénouement; they hold, each in their own way, additional surprises for the reader. . . .

A Departure for Cormier

In rather dramatic contrast to *After the First Death* is Cormier's *Eight Plus One*, a collection of short stories originally published between 1965 and 1975 in magazines such. as *Redbook*, *Woman's Day*, *McCall's*, and the *Saturday Evening Post*. . . .

Cormier explains the title for this collection: Eight stories have teenagers as the central figures and involve the strengthening of family bonds; in the final story—the "one" of the title—the children are only in the background of the life of a man who plans to leave his wife of many years and their children for a much younger woman. . . .

Eight Plus One can be grimly realistic and bleak—although not all the stories could be so described—but in this collection, as in the novels, Cormier refuses to take the popular, sentimental, easy way out. This book has received less critical acclaim than the novels, but the American Library Association has included *Eight Plus One* on its list of Notable Books in the Field of Social Studies.

Cormier's next novel, *The Bumblebee Flies Anyway*, published in 1983, is set in Section 12 of the Complex, the wing for terminally ill youths in an experimental hospital. The author has revealed that the catalysts for this novel were a poster of a bumblebee that he has had for many years in his writing room and his reading about experimental hospitals.

Barney Snow, sixteen, whose surname connotes his innocence, is the narrator. Barney's role is to unite the others: Ronson, a Golden Gloves winner; Allie Roon, with an old man's face, spastic and stammering; Billy the Kidney, wheelchair bound but desirous of adventure; and Alberto "Mazzo" Mazzofono, rich, handsome, athletic, but plugged into a machine. This unlikely cast of characters is brought together by their volunteering to spend their last days as subjects for a study of experimental drugs and techniques which will not save them but will perhaps help someone, someday.

The Bumblebee is a life-size model of a red MG [a British sports car], made of wood, symbolizing the dreams of the others that Barney strives to help them achieve. They will "fly" in the Bumblebee, so named by Mazzo's twin sister, Cassie, after the heavy-bodied, short-winged bee who, aerodynamically speaking, should not be able to lift itself off the ground, but who, blissfully unaware of any such concept, flies anyway. At the heart of this pessimistic, depressing scene of dying teenagers stands Cormier's message to follow one's dreams, to dare to fly. . . .

Continued Success

Also well received was *Beyond the Chocolate War*, Cormier's sequel to the earlier novel. Published in 1985, eleven years after *The Chocolate War*, this novel moves at the same relentless pace as its predecessor. Indeed, Cormier rewrites and revises constantly to achieve his pacing with its gradual disclosure. Cormier has said that questions from readers about Archie or Jerry or even Tubs Casper, which kept the characters alive for him, and his own curiosity about Obie, whom he sees as a tragic but terrific character, were the impetuses for the writing of this novel.

Beyond the Chocolate War has received mostly favorable reviews; any unfavorable commentary apparently stems from a comparison with Cormier's earlier novel as the standard. For example, Hazel Rochman in the *New York Times Book Review* describes it as "not as starkly dramatic as its predecessor," and Roger Sutton in *School Library Journal* believes that "as a whole this is less compelling as fiction than it is as a commentary on *The Chocolate War*—Cormier here intensifies and explicates what was powerfully implicit in the first book." Awards include *Horn Book*'s listing it in "Fanfare," *Parents' Choice* including it among their remarkable books, and the *New York Times* naming it a Notable Book of the Year for 1985. . . .

In November 1988, *Fade*, one of Cormier's most sophisticated books, appeared. Spanning three generations and set primarily in Frenchtown, the French Canadian section of Monument, the novel centers on Paul Moreaux, who has inherited the ability to fade or become invisible, a characteristic occurring in the Moreaux family once a generation and passed from uncle to nephew. A fader can recognize another fader and is able to sense the presence of another; he is also able to intuit the proper time to seek out the young one in adolescence and educate him about his "power." Uncle Adelard, the fader of the previous generation, cautions Paul about the misuse of power just as Paul will later try to warn his nephew, Ozzie Slater, about the power.

The fade has been interpreted in various ways—as evil, or even as original sin. At first a blessing, it becomes a curse. Its power enables Paul to escape from danger of attack by a Ku Klux Klan member and later by a bully, but it also enables him to observe some sexual acts, shocking to him and perhaps to the teenage reader as well. The fade or lust for power or evil gradually assumes control over the fader until acts of violence and several murders are perpetrated and the fader's life changed irrevocably. Paul vows after an act of revenge not to use the fade again, and he does not until he feels he must to prove to his nephew that he possesses the ability. . . .

One topic new to the Cormier canon in this novel is the development of a writer. Not only do readers gain insight about Paul Roget as the author of *Bruises in Paradise, Come Home, Come Home,* and *Dialogue at Midnight,* as well as the Paul Moreaux manuscript, but they also become intimately involved with Susan Roget as she struggles to become a writer, quoting a professor's directions on how to begin, on being oneself, and on being willing to take risks. Even the problems of editors are presented, such as Meredith quoting Paul Roget that a novelist is permitted "one major coincidence" in a book, and the pains and difficulties confronting editors in verifying details.

Autobiographical Elements

Fade contains many autobiographical elements, and Paul, by Cormier's own admission, is his most autobiographical character. In an article in *Horn Book* titled "Creating *Fade*," Cormier describes the photograph of his father's family, with one missing uncle, that provided one impetus for the novel. Another was the need to look back, to recapture a time in the past during which he spent two and a half years writing the novel which would later be revised to half its original length. In the 1963 section of Paul's manuscript the scenes between Paul and his father are reminiscent of those between Cormier and his father; he found them especially painful to cut, but they were greatly shortened. Some other autobiographical elements are Paul's desire to be a writer, his attitude toward Catholicism, his paper route, his conflict with a bully, and his crushes on females. Paul's cousin Susan is modeled somewhat after Cormier's youngest child, Renee. . . .

In a departure from his regular audience, Cormier wrote *Other Bells for Us to Ring* in 1990 for a younger group, although critics disagree on the exact ages it was intended for: some suggest as young as eight, and others suggest thirteen and older. The title of the book was originally *Darcy*; Cormier's American editor, preferring to avoid name titles, encouraged him to change it and he did, but in England it was published as *Darcy*. The genesis of the novel was an incident revealed to Cormier's wife by an elderly lady named Hazel Heald. As a young Protestant girl, Hazel was sprinkled with holy water in a Catholic church by a young friend who announced that she was now a Catholic. Hazel was horrified and ran to her mother, who assured her that she was not a Catholic. Cormier dedicates the book to Hazel Heald and to his grandchildren. . . .

Publishing into the 1990s

We All Fall Down [1991] is a complex but fascinating study of adolescence. Its impetus was a news clipping about an incidence of vandalism in a Boston suburb. Cormier was struck by the fact that the perpetrators were not thugs; they were middle-class kids, yet they did unspeakable things to the house. He wanted to explore the point of view of one of the vandals and at the same time the point of view of one of the girls whose home had been destroyed.

The novel, set in Burnside, a neighboring community of Monument, is actually told from the points of view of three characters: Buddy Walker, one of the vandals; Jane Jerome, older sister of Karen Jerome, who lies in a coma as a result of the trashing of her home; and the Avenger, whose identity is not revealed until the final pages.

Themes of gang action, alcoholism, and divorce center around teenager Buddy Walker, who turns to alcohol for consolation when his father announces a divorce and his mother is left numb. Neglected by his parents, vulnerable, and lonely, he becomes prey to vicious Harry Flowers, leader of a gang of four who trashes the Jerome house in Burnside. Buddy participates in the action while drunk. Fourteen-year-old Karen Jerome comes home unexpectedly and is almost raped, but then is pushed down a flight of stairs and ends up in a coma. Buddy is the only one of the four who feels contrite. . . .

The impetus for *Tunes for Bears to Dance To* (1992), a novel for younger teens, was a recreated village carved for a craft show by an old Italian woodcarver, who spoke of his art with great emotional intensity. Cormier wondered what would happen if that work were smashed. He also wondered what would happen if an eleven-year-old were tempted into destroying the village by a corrupt older man, perhaps a grocer.

Cormier had once worked for a grocer, who was not evil, but rather was a practical joker. Cormier chose to focus on eleven-year-olds here and in many of his other novels because they are at a difficult stage—not yet into puberty, but not really children either.

This short novel, almost a morality tale, examines evil and its power to corrupt. . . .

Cormier's next book, *In the Middle of the Night* (1995), was selected by the American Library Association as a Best Book for Young Adults as well as a Quick Pick in 1995. Nominated for the Edgar Award by the Mystery Writers of America in 1995 and for the California Reader Medal in 1995–1996, the book explores many of Cormier's previous themes but adds a new look at the themes of guilt and of the sins of the fathers visited upon the children.

The idea of a disaster being revisited on its anniversary came to Cormier as he read the yearly recounting of the famous Coconut Grove nightclub fire which happened in Boston in 1942. Almost five hundred people lost their lives when they could not escape from the overcrowded building. A busboy who lit a match was at first blamed for the disaster but later exonerated. Cormier wanted to examine what would happen to people caught in such a disaster and its aftereffects on a second generation. . . .

Although Cormier claims that he gets his plots from serendipity, he works hard writing and rewriting, often discarding hundreds of pages as he did from *Beyond the Chocolate War* and *Fade*. His work proves his versatility. Avid fans in many countries have purchased millions of copies of his books. He has traveled extensively, speaking to and listening to young adults in most of the fifty states, as well as in Australia, England, and Scotland. He said in a 23 May 1989 personal letter that "teenagers are teenagers all over the world and sitting on school steps in Melbourne with thirteen and fourteen year olds, I could have been in Boston, Massachusetts, or Edinburgh, Scotland." Cormier has acquired these fans because of his sensitive awareness about what actually occurs in the lives of teenagers today and his abundant talent for conveying that awareness through fiction. He has brought controversy and, simultaneously, a new dimension to the field of young-adult literature. He has earned the respect of his readers, regardless of their age, because of his refusal to compromise the truth as he sees it. His superb craftsmanship, his ability to create suspense and to shock the reader repeatedly, and his forcing the reader to think are all qualities which make Cormier's works entertaining, unique, and, indeed, unforgettable.

The Chocolate War
Was Inspired by an Event
in Cormier's Life

Robert Cormier, Interviewed by John Cohen

John Cohen is an editor for Reading Time.

In this interview with John Cohen, Cormier talks about the genesis of The Chocolate War. *There was a chocolate sale at his son Peter's school, and the Cormier family made the decision that Peter did not have to sell the chocolates. Cormier states that he is a very emotional writer, so he began writing about what could have happened to his son following this act of defiance.* The Chocolate War *was Cormier's first young-adult novel and launched his career in that genre.*

John Cohen: Robert, I first came across your first major work for young people, The Chocolate War, *in 1974 when I was in the United States. It had just been released and of course it was the talk of the town. What triggered that particular story off?*

Robert Cormier: I woke up one day to find myself as a young adult author, but what triggered it really was a very personal thing. My son went to a Catholic private boys' school of 400 boys and they were having a chocolate sale. He came home one day with two shopping bags of boxes to sell, which dismayed me in a way because I went through a parochial school system in the depression where times were hard and we sold everything to help support the purchase of the basic needs of the school. I remember nuns even crocheting the edges of hankies for sale. Now here we are a generation later, times being pretty good to us, a middle class family, paying tuition at a school, and I thought, "My God, what are we doing with a chocolate sale at this point?" The upshot of it all was that we made a family decision with my son, Peter, that he would not sell the chocolates. This is fine when you are talking about it but when it actually goes into practice it has an entirely different aspect.

An Emotional Writer

I am an emotional writer in that I do not write emotionally but if something affects me emotionally then that sends me to the typewriter. I don't devise a plot and then start writing but the emotions with this issue were amazing because I took him to school the next day with his chocolates and a letter to his headmaster saying that he wouldn't be taking part in the sale as a matter of principle and he had the approval and support of his parents. When he got out of the car and went up the walk I realized the truth, first of all it was just before the bell rang and 400 athletic, energetic boys were jostling each other. Peter walked up with his bags and I realized he was 14 years old: this was the start of the school year; he was in a new school in a new city and he was virtually with 399 strangers. He looked so vulnerable and I wondered what is going to happen to him. I thought that they would probably kill him. These were the first words of *The Chocolate War*, "They murdered him", so it sent me to the typewriter. Peter had no problems. In fact we would not have allowed him to get into this situation if he was extra sensitive or an introvert, but he was an average kid who played football, was a B student, got along well and didn't seem to have any problems. I worried about it at first when he walked up that walk, thinking that we were going to ruin his high school career. Actually the kids were OK with him and they only kidded him a little bit. Ironically the brother who was in charge of the school was his home room teacher and everyday, just as was in the book, there was a roll call and every day the teacher asked the students one by one, how many chocolates they had sold the day before. For five weeks Peter said, "None." He confessed towards the end that he thought the teacher was getting a little tense about it, but nothing more than that happened. However, as a writer, I started thinking what if there had been peer pressure and faculty pressure and so I began to write what became *The Chocolate War*. My agent called me to say she hadn't heard from me. I told her I was writing this crazy thing about chocolates and the sale and about a boy who goes to high school and she said it sounds like a YA novel and I asked her, "What's a YA novel?" She said "A Young Adult novel, a wonderful new series of books coming out in the schools. It makes a nice bridge from the kind of books the kids brought into the class to the classics," and of course she scared me to death because I thought I would have to go back and see what I have been writing here. I hadn't been conscious of using anything that would affront anybody. I was writing about the way boys act and talk, think of girls and about masturbation. She said not to worry about all of that but just write this book as I saw it and let her worry about the publishing, so that is what I did. I found that the young people who were led to my books by teachers and librarians were a terrific audience and I could write for them with all the craft I could summon. I always had the very intelligent reader in mind who happened to turn out to be a 13-year-old reader sometimes. So that is the genesis [of *The Chocolate War*].

Robert Cormier Wrote
The Chocolate War from
His Emotions

Robert Cormier, Interviewed by Geraldine DeLuca and Roni Natov

Geraldine DeLuca and Roni Natov were the cofounding editors of The Lion and the Unicorn, *which they coedited until 1993. DeLuca is a professor of English at New York University and writes widely in the field of children's literature. Natov is a professor of English at Brooklyn College.*

In this interview with Geraldine DeLuca and Roni Natov, Robert Cormier talks about the event in his son's life that inspired The Chocolate War *and caused him to begin writing young-adult fiction. Like the earlier adult novels he had written,* The Chocolate War *is his emotional response to an event in his life.*

Geraldine DeLuca: Why did you start to write for adolescents?

Robert Cormier: Well, I didn't start writing specifically for adolescents. I was surrounded by my kids and their friends who were teenagers, and I realized that they were really leading a life that was more exciting than mine. I was going to work every day and coming back home, but for them the emotional pendulum was swinging back and forth all the time. They were getting invited to the prom, falling in love—you know those things—and even though the experiences might have been transient, they were really lacerating for them. So I began to write short stories about young people. They appeared in magazines, not as young adults' stories, but in *Redbook, Saturday Evening Post, McCall's,* and they were

Geraldine DeLuca and Roni Natov, "An Interview with Robert Cormier," *The Lion and the Unicorn*, vol. 2, no. 2, Fall 1978, pp. 109–35. Reproduced by permission.

usually about a relationship between a father and a daughter or a father and a son. So the next step seemed to be . . . to a novel.

I didn't look for it, but what happened was, my son was a freshman in this jock boys' Catholic high school and he came home with chocolates to sell. He wanted to play football and he's an average student so he knew he had to do a lot of homework and then suddenly he also had to sell these chocolates. It reminded me of the Depression when all of us sold everything in a Catholic school—chocolates, candy, greeting cards, chances—and I thought, "How far have we come in a generation?" He's going to a Catholic prep school, we're paying tuition, and he's still selling chocolates. So we kidded around about it in the evening, you know, like families do over the dinner table. And suddenly I said, "You know, Peter, there are options available. You don't have to sell the chocolates. One option is that we can buy them—there were twenty-five boxes at a dollar apiece and I was hoping he wouldn't say 'Yeah, Fine'—or you can not sell them." And he decided that he wouldn't sell them. We figured as a family we'd take a stand.

The Emotions Kick In

So I wrote a letter to his headmaster to say that he wasn't doing this frivolously, that we had thought about it, that it was a free society and that his option was not to sell the chocolates. So the next day he had to bring the chocolates back. I said, "Well, you won't go on the bus with two bags. I'll take you to school." And as I let him go up the walk with the two bags I thought, "God, what am I letting him in for?" Because he was a freshman, and it was only the end of September in this very active school. I felt kind of guilty about it. And that's where the emotions came from to allow me to write about it, because I do write from the emotions. So, what happened is, he gave the letter to the headmaster, who read it and said "Fine,

Peter," and nothing happened. The kids later kidded him a little bit, the way kids do, but the emotions started growing in me.

Then I started to explore the situation, you know the old crutches that we all have: "What if?" What if the headmaster hadn't been that understanding? And then, what if the chocolate sale was very important to his school? And then, what if he had peer pressure?" So I started writing about this situation, and frankly, the boy at that point was Peter, my son, and the school was his school. So I just wrote, because I write every day—it's part of the fabric of my life. When I got about a third into what became *The Chocolate War*, my agent asked me, "What have you been doing lately, I haven't heard from you?" and I said, "I don't know, Marilyn [Marlow], I'm writing this crazy thing about kids selling chocolate in high school and I'm not sure what I've got." So I sent her what I had and she called back and said, "You know, this sounds like a young adult novel." This was the first time I really thought of it as a young adult novel or thought of a young adult novel as something that people really read. I knew vaguely that writers wrote books for children, but I didn't know about the young adult market. I didn't know about [famed young-adult author] Paul Zindel. But she sort of scared me when she said that. I thought, "Oh, my God, do I have to go back and simplify and take things out?" I didn't even know what kind of language was in it. But she said, "Bob, don't worry about it. Just write as you were writing before, and let me determine the market." . . .

Roni Natov: It's very interesting. There's so much energy in this book. I keep feeling that it must come from something that did happen or that you were afraid would happen. The story is very intense and I think that's what makes it feel authentic. It doesn't feel like the typical young adult novel sort of trumped up to air issues or to solve problems.

An Emotional Writer

Cormier: I was exploring. I should go back to what I said about the emotions. I've always been an emotional writer, which has been both good and bad for my career. It's been bad for my career because I've been led into unpopular themes. If I sat down and just wanted to construct something I thought would sell, things might have been easier. My first novel, *Now and At the Hour*, was about a man dying of cancer and this was back fifteen years ago when death was not "in." It may seem strange to say that but death is now studied in college seminars. My second novel, *A Little Raw on Monday Mornings*, was about a middle-aged, Catholic woman involved in an abortion problem at a time when abortion wasn't the Sunday Supplement kind of subject it is today. But I was led to those novels through emotion. My father died of cancer and I was very close to him, so I wrote out of that experience. . . .

So when I came to *The Chocolate War* I was exploring these emotions and situations rather than worrying about the market or "examining the theme of the individual against society," even though I'd always been interested in that. When people read it, they impose these ideas on it. Critics say, "This is a novel about the individual against society." And I say, "That's right, it is." But I didn't say, "I'm going to sit down and explore this." There are patterns in my work. Like the old man running away, I realized, looking back, that there has always been a pattern. In a very small way, I am sometimes a rebel myself without anybody knowing about it.

DeLuca: Do you think that the odds against the individual surviving are as great as your books suggest?

Cormier: Well, yes. I don't think that there are always happy endings, but you can get satisfaction out of experiences even though you fail. Like [in Ernest Hemingway's] *The Old Man and the Sea*. The sharks tore the marlin a part, so he failed in one sense. Yet, it was a great story of fulfillment. I know people feel my books are depressing and I suppose *The Chocolate War* is depressing because, at the end, Jerry is apparently defeated and I couldn't help that. When I began writing it, I just wanted to set the situation up and then the characters became real to me. In every story, once an author has established the people and the situations, there's an air of inevitability about it that can't be tampered with. You know, one day while I was sitting at home, I got a phone call from Marilyn who had heard from the second editor. He had said, "Fine, it's great." If I would change the ending, they would buy the book. Now I had no way of knowing that Pantheon would eventually buy the book as is and that it would sell. And here was this editor saying, "It's great. However, we don't think young people will accept it." Well, first of all, that raised my hackles.

Natov: It's like, *sell the chocolates!*

Cormier: That's right. He was doing the same thing. And yet it was very tempting to say, "Well, let me see about it." But I knew that in my mind the curve of the story was to build and then go down. And I had this crazy image in my mind of trying to fix up the ending to make it go up—"zip"—which seemed untrue, but it was tempting.

Staying True to the Story

Now when Pantheon accepted it, Fabio, my editor, suggested a change that was very effective. In the first version of the fight, Jerry was annihilated immediately, because I didn't think I could sustain the raffle idea, and thought I'd better get rid of the fight quickly. But Fabio said, "I think for reader response and for balance you should think about prolonging the fight to let Jerry get in a little more." He said, as all good editors say, "Think about it." So I thought about it and said, yes, I could see where it was an abbreviated fight. I had built it up and then it was over like that. Artistically I felt it could go longer and I tried it. So Jerry did get in a couple of licks and yet the inevitability of the story imposed itself, because when he did, he realized he was lowering himself to Janza's level. So again, the truth of the book was sustained. I believe in this sense of inevitability. And when I'm bothered by a book that I read that doesn't ring true, I wonder whether the author, playing God, didn't tamper somewhere, by not following the natural outcome.

DeLuca: That's interesting. I remember this book being discussed once at a children's literature conference where one of the women kept insisting that it was just like *Hamlet*. And you do make references to Shakespeare, so I was wondering if you have a sense of the inevitability being tragic, of the options becoming narrower and narrower for Jerry.

Cormier: No, it's funny. Lou Willett Stanek, who did the Dell teacher's guide for both *The Chocolate War* and *I Am the Cheese*, made all these Shakespearean references, comparing *The Chocolate War* to *Hamlet*. She likened the conversation between Archie and Obie to that between Rosencrantz and Guildenstern. So I was pleased. I thought, what a comparison! But I wasn't conscious of it when I was writing. I was conscious, of course, of using [T.S.] Eliot's line from "[The Love Song of J. Alfred] Prufrock": "Do I dare disturb the universe?" Which is essentially a middle-aged man's question, because that's what Prufrock was. And yet, you can disturb the universe on all levels.

Natov: I also felt that Jerry was identifying and worrying about identifying with his father there. His father was so bleak, so defeated, and he was wondering, "Is there any other way? Do I dare do something else?"

Cormier: Yes, there were circumstances that dictated his rebellion, more than he realized. There's the scene early in the book with the hippie who comes across the street and says, "Go back to your closed little world," and his father's world *was* closed. There was a time, I remember, when I was that age, that I'd go out after supper and the place I wanted to be was out of the house, seeing what was going on downtown on the street corner. And I'd see my father taking a nap after supper, after working all day, and I'd think, "My goodness, is this all he has to live for?" Now, of course, I take naps after supper. And when my own son is going out I think, "Thank God, the search is over for me." I don't have to search those streets for love and so forth. So this generation repeats. If I have total recall of anything, it's of my emotions when I was young. My youngest daughter, who's now eleven, said something once which delighted me. She was nine or ten at the time—the age when they think their father's a giant, you know. It's too bad she'll be leaving that soon, and she'll realize my feet are clay. But she said to me, "You know what I like about you, Dad? You remember what it was like when you were young." And I realized that that was true. I can recall those emotions of adolescence pretty well and apparently it comes out in the books, because kids write me marvelous letters. So apparently, I do have that recall. And I don't worry too much about trends or styles. I figure that if the emotions are right, the response will be there. It seems to have worked so far.

The Chocolate War and Its Antagonists

Natov: I'm interested in the connection between power and guilt, and shame and fear in your work. They seem to be all tied up in *The Chocolate War*. Archie's power comes from understanding, in some very intense way, that other people are ashamed of things. He could know that through his own feelings—he knows about shame, he knows about guilt, and he knows what to do about it. Were you conscious of the different things that people, that teenagers, hide, and that this huge figure, Archie, is trying to uncover and use? Like the incident of Janza in the bathroom?

Cormier: I've been aware of people like this all my life. There are people who can intimidate other people very easily and I've always been interested in why they can do it. I think it's because most people want peace. You know, you get on a bus and just want to take your ride quietly, but there are some people who just don't want that quiet ride. And when they find out that other people want peace, they can intimidate them because of that. Just a short while ago I was standing in line at a theater and the line was sort of crooked so that someone could come in. So someone came in and stood right in front of me. Or there's the person who double parks his car to go into a store, knowing he's blocking another person, and not seeming to care that that person might come out while he's in the store. Do you see what I mean? It's a million of these little things that I'm aware of.

I knew, when I started the book, that eventually there had to be a confrontation between the good guys and the bad guys, between Jerry and Archie. And I didn't know then who would win and who would lose, I just knew there had to be a showdown. I introduced this fellow named Emile Janza in order to show Archie in a different light. You know, not to show him from the point of view of someone he'd been intimidating, but to show him through the eyes of a guy who was almost at his level, but not that sharp. So that's all Janza was. But he kept popping up, I found him very convenient, and suddenly I found him growing. And part of the joy of writing, at least the way I do it, is that suddenly I had this full-blown character on my hands, and it made me realize that Archie would never risk a confrontation with anyone. He would have Janza do it. And this is what I mean about setting your characters in motion. If I had insisted, as an author, that I had wanted Archie in that ring with Jerry, I don't think it would have rung true because Archie wouldn't have done it. But I didn't know that at the beginning of the story. Of course, there is danger in this too. You can be carried away by people who throw your book off, and sometimes you have to go back and cut. Amy, for example, almost ran away with *I Am the Cheese* because I fell madly in love with her, and then I just had to eliminate her.

Sins of Commission and Omission

Natov: She's appealing, I can see it.

Cormier: Yes, she really captured me. I went on and on about her and then I just had to just throw those pages away because she didn't belong.

So there are people who use power in a very small way because they know that most of us want to go along and just live our lives. I have met people like that.

DeLuca: They don't have any satisfaction within themselves and the only way they can get any is to provoke hostility in others. Archie's like that. The only thing that seems to give him any pleasure is manipulating others, making them feel as wretched as he feels. It's the same thing with Brother Leon. He's such an unhappy character.

Cormier: Yes, their own unhappiness comes back. And I feel that they're not prototypes; I hope they're just individuals. However, there are Brother Leons in schools everywhere.

Natov: He felt totally insidious. He's a very dangerous person because he is an adult. More dangerous than Archie.

DeLuca: And he's not dealing with other adults, he's dealing with kids, who are more vulnerable.

Cormier: Yes. There is that scene in the classroom where he manipulates Gregory Bailey. And yet that scene is also about the guilt of all of us. You know, the biggest sins in the world are not so much the sins of commission, as the sins of omission. I think about how many times I've stood in mixed company while somebody told a real dirty joke, and I didn't say anything, didn't say, "Look, why did you tell that?" That's the sort of guilt I wanted to show—how we all collaborate in these situations. I started out writing that chapter to show how terrible Brother Leon was and then in the writing I suddenly realized, "My God, the class is as guilty at this moment as he is."

DeLuca: Except that they're very vulnerable.

Cormier: Except that they're very vulnerable, yes. And they are intimidated by it. Again, intimidation can reduce people to do things they don't want to do. Or to do things collectively that they wouldn't do alone. So if you're going to fight this kind of thing, you've got to be collectively good. Most people have missed this. The fact is there was only one good person in the book.

DeLuca: There's Goober and there's Brother Jacques.

Cormier: But they're weak, ineffectual. If they were collective, if they banded as the evildoers did, they would have had some power.

High School as Metaphor for Society

DeLuca: Were you aware of how bleak a vision you were presenting? Did you feel that this school was in some way a microcosm?

Cormier: No. As I went along I was aware that I was exploring things. And it occurred to me at one point that this high school was really a metaphor, that I could just as well be writing about someone in business who refused to conform, probably in a place like this, where everybody had to wear a tie all the time and one guy decided not to. And I realized that that's why I didn't think of it as a young adult novel. I thought it was more than just a book for young people. I was hoping that even though most of the characters were youngsters, older people would get shocks of recognition and say, "Yes, I remember how it was."

Natov: How it *is*.

Cormier: How it is. And how it was for them when they were young.

DeLuca: You have those scenes where kids band together and taunt other kids, which you see more openly among adolescents and children than you do among adults—it's much more subtle among adults.

45

Cormier: Yes. You know, what astounded me was that some people got upset and said they couldn't accept that kids would do this. But really, children are the cruelest of all, because they haven't entered society yet and realized that if you want to make a living you've got to get along. Some schools have refused to have *The Chocolate War* because they feel it's a bad portrait of youth. I don't know what their motivations are, but . . .

Natov: It's not a very positive portrait of the Catholic school.

Cormier: It isn't. And there has been controversy about that, but I have had very little complaint from Catholics.

DeLuca: Are you a Catholic?

Cormier: Yes, I'm a Catholic, and I went to those kinds of schools. But I was writing about a specific situation here. I had a horrible time in parochial school and I also had a great time, you know? When an advance review came out, it said the book would be very controversial, especially among Catholics. But I spoke at the Catholic Library Association in St. Louis a couple of months ago and we had a very good time. A couple of people there did tell me, though, that they are librarians in Catholic schools and they don't have it on the shelves. However, in the school my son went to, the book has achieved a sort of legendary status. My son had a friend who is a runner, and he claims he's the Goober. Nobody claims they're Archie; they all claim they're either the Goober or Jerry.

You know, the funny thing about writing is that it is such a private act and it becomes such a public thing. When I was writing, I was just trying to find a specific truth. I was once asked at a seminar, "Why did you make it Catholic? You said it could happen in any school; there are Brother Leons in public schools, in private schools and in parochial schools, so why did you make it Catholic?" And I said, "Well, you've got to be specific."

A Unique Setting Can Be Universal

Natov: You've got to make it *something*.

Cormier: You've got to make it something. You know, if I just made it a bland school somewhere, then the next thing to say would be, well I'd better not make this kid French. I'd better not make this one Italian. I'd better not make this one Irish. And you end up with homogenized milk. So once I made the decision to make it a Catholic school, I hoped readers would see that it's universal, that these people exist everywhere.

Natov: I feel like it had something to do with its being a boy's school, though. There's something frenetic going on there.

Cormier: Yes. There's something about a boy's school. As I said, my son was going to this school and it was a jock school and it was—frenetic is a beautiful word for it. The chocolate sale there is a real annual thing in the town and people sort of know it's coming. But I never heard a word of criticism about the book from the school. In fact my son helped me. I had him check out the teenage slang. He'd say things like, "They don't say 'broads' anymore, Dad, they say 'chicks.'" Things like that. But anyway, when the book was done and he was still there, I told him that if it would embarrass him I wouldn't send it in. Because I was always writing other things. I said I'd wait until he was out of the place. But he said, "Dad, it wouldn't bother me at all." In fact, he's that kind of kid. That's why I didn't have too many misgivings about letting him go against the grain. Some sensitive, introverted boy I wouldn't have exposed to that type of situation. But he was as much of a jock as all the rest of the boys, so I figured it wouldn't bother him.

DeLuca: It's interesting, though, that the characters in your books don't have support from their parents the way your son has. The parents are dead or in some way rendered impotent. And they're very separate from their children.

Cormier: Yes. Well, you know, about the only father who appeared in *The Chocolate War* was Jerry's father and he was indifferent because of his grief about his wife's death. I did that purposely. I have a private belief—and like all beliefs it's not total—but I have the feeling we should judge people more often on what they do rather than excusing them for coming from unhappy homes. I think the essential individual, the true thing that a person is, probably does not have a lot to do with where he comes from. I may be wrong. I've argued a lot about this and I'm always willing to concede. I don't mean to say that people who come from a very hard background don't have it hard. What I mean is that there is a spirit of a person, you know? So I purposely left out all families—there are no other mothers and fathers around—because I wanted the boys to be judged on what they did, not "why did Archie do that?"

Natov: Yes, I noticed there was no attempt to psychoanalyze Archie.

Cormier: People can't say Archie did this because he was a deprived child or he was a victim of child abuse. I wanted him judged solely on his actions. So that's why Jerry's father was the only one. And he was more or less ineffective because of his own sorrow. He wasn't that vital a character anyway, or he wouldn't have been that devastated.

DeLuca: People do notice though that Jerry doesn't have that support, that his father is not aware that he is getting beat up, that he's unhappy, that people are calling him and threatening him. If some adult figure had been there to say something, the outcome might have been different. . . .

The Chocolate War Is a Page-Turner

DeLuca: Your books are beautifully written. Adolescent novels tend not to be very well written and these really stand out, *The Chocolate War* particularly.

Cormier: Well, thank you. I love to hear that, naturally.

Natov: Oh, we'll say more. The dialogue is wonderful in *The Chocolate War*, very inventive. Each character has a clear voice.

Cormier: I love to hear that because I'm a frustrated script writer, screen writer, I think. I love writing dialogue.

Natov: I can see it, because the books are dramas. They're not novels of sensibility. The characters collide, things happen, they are constantly talking to each other. Even when they're talking in their heads, they're talking out whole scenarios.

Cormier: Yes, I write cinematically but try to keep that forward thrust. I want to keep the reader turning those pages. I'm conscious of the reader. And I try to write the way I would like to read a book, so I create incident and conflicts. Rather than waiting for one big climax, I try to create a lot of little conflicts between people. Part of that comes from my short story training where you have to get quick climaxes in a short space of time, rather than waiting until the middle of the book for a great one. I try to create a series of explosions as I go along.

DeLuca: The opening line of *The Chocolate War* is explosive: "They murdered him."

Cormier: Yes. I had a call from some kids down in South Carolina. They were at school and their teacher gave them permission to call me. They were calling from a corridor apparently—I could hear them talking—and they were having a big argument. Half the class said that Jerry died at the end, because I had said at the beginning that they murdered him and they took it literally. And the other half said he didn't, so they asked, "What do you think?" And I said, "Well, in my own mind, he's still alive," so one kid says, "Great! Now will you tell this other guy here so he'll hear you?" So I said, "Well, I'll do better than that. Give me your address." So I wrote to them. It's terrific to get this kind of feedback, to have kids care enough to have a big argument. It must have delighted the teacher, and it's a delight for me to think that they're taking what is probably a very downbeat book, which has caused controversy, and getting something out of it. You know, it's better than arguing about what [1970s TV series characters] Starsky and Hutch did last night!

Robert Cormier Explains His Pessimism

Robert Cormier

Robert Cormier was an award-winning writer known for such novels as I Am the Cheese, Fade, After the First Death, *and* Beyond the Chocolate War.

In an article appearing in Publishers Weekly, *Cormier explains why he can write about such terrible topics as sadism, murder, torture, terrorism, and suicide and still be a man who "longs for happy endings." He admits that he develops an affection for many of his characters as he writes about them and that it pains him when he knows that the circumstances of the novel mean they must die. Novels need to explore all aspects of human nature, Cormier insists, including those that disturb us.*

In a single paragraph of an article dealing with *The Chocolate War, I Am the Cheese,* and *After the First Death*, a writer listed these topics as central to the books: brutality, sadism, corruption (religious and governmental), insanity, murder, torture, personality destruction, terrorism, child murder, and suicide.

What kind of person writes about those terrible things? And why?

The name on the novels is Robert Cormier, and my name is Robert Cormier. But sometimes I don't recognize myself, either in what others say about my work or when I face questions from an audience about the violent nature of the books that bear my name.

A Personality Paradox Explained

I am a man who cries at sad movies, longs for happy endings, delights in atrocious puns, pauses to gather branches of bittersweet at the side of a highway. I am shamelessly sentimental: I always make a wish when I blow out the candles on my birthday cake, and I dread the day when there may be no one there to say "Bless you" when I sneeze. Although I aspire to be Superman, I am doomed to be Clark Kent forever, in an endless search for that magic telephone booth. I wear a trench coat, but nobody ever mistakes me for Humphrey Bogart. I hesitate to kill a fly—but people die horrible deaths in my novels.

But, of course, it's easy to kill off characters in novels or assign them tragic roles, because they are only figments of the imagination. People in books are made of print and paper, not flesh and blood, after all. They are creatures who live and die only between the covers of a book. Right?

Wrong. They also live in my mind and imagination and have the power to disturb dreams and to invoke themselves at odd, unguarded moments. Kate Forrester in *After the First Death* was a very real person to me. I cheered her brave actions as they unfolded on the page. I was moved by her sense of responsibility toward the children who were hostages on that hijacked bus. I loved the way she refused to concede defeat. And yet, I sensed a doom descending on her, a foreshadowing of failure. She was an amateur at deceit and intrigue. And amateurs often make mistakes, fatal miscalculations. In going to the limit of her dwindling resources to protect the children and then to escape, it was inevitable that she would go too far. I saw her moving in that direction with the horror that a parent feels watching a child dash into noonday traffic on a busy street, helpless to avert what must happen.

Fiction must follow an internal logic. Given the circumstances I had created, Kate had to die. That doesn't mean I didn't mourn—or that I don't wish to write happier stories, with strolling-into-sunset endings, the cavalry arriving at the last minute. How I loved the sound of bugles and those thundering hooves at Saturday movie matinees.

But I've come to realize that Saturday matinees have nothing to do with real life, that innocence doesn't provide immunity from evil, that the mugger lurking in the doorway assaults both the just and the unjust.

It is possible to be a peaceful man, to abhor violence, to love children and flowers and old Beatles songs, and still be aware of the contusions and abrasions this world inflicts on us. Not to write happy endings doesn't mean the writer doesn't believe in them. Literature should penetrate all the chambers of the human heart, even the dark ones.

Cormier Broke New Ground with Honest, Realistic Young-Adult Fiction

Patty Campbell

Patty Campbell is the author of the most highly regarded biography of Cormier, Presenting Robert Cormier.

In this tribute to Cormier written at the time of his death, Patty Campbell recognizes him as the leading writer in the field of young-adult fiction. She praises Cormier's writing for his suspenseful plots, cinematic technique, serious subjects, and somber themes, which he confronts with uncompromising honesty.

Young adult [YA] literature has lost its grand master. On November 2, 2000, Robert Cormier died in Boston after a brief illness. He was seventy-five years old, but his thirteen YA novels speak to the hearts of teens everywhere and will continue to do so for many years to come. Cormier was acknowledged as the finest writer in the genre—and also the first to show the literary world that YA novels could be not only realistic about teen concerns but unflinchingly honest about big questions like the abuse of power, courage, forgiveness and redemption, and the struggle to stay human in a world that is, as [*Chronicles of Narnia* author] C.S. Lewis has called it, "enemy-occupied territory." While the daring of his subjects has often drawn censorship attacks, the brilliance of his writing earned him many literary prizes. He was the recipient of the American Library Association's Margaret A. Edwards Award in 1991 and of the ALAN Award of the National Council of Teachers of English in 1982, both given for lifetime achievement in young adult literature, as well as many other honors, both national and international.

Patty Campbell, "A Loving Farewell to Robert Cormier," *The Horn Book Magazine*, vol. 77, no. 2, March 2001, p. 245–248. Copyright © 2001 by The Horn Book, Inc., Boston, MA, www.hbook.com. All rights reserved. Reproduced by permission.

The Chocolate War
Transformed YA Literature

The publication in 1974 of Cormier's first YA novel, *The Chocolate War*, initiated a new level of literary excellence in the fledgling genre of young adult fiction. It also began a storm of controversy about the darkness and hard truth-telling of his work that continues to this day. The critical dialogue generated by *The Chocolate War* led to recognition not only of Cormier's gifts but also of the young adult novel by the literary establishment. As critic and YA author Michael Cart said in the *Los Angeles Times*, Cormier "single-handedly . . . transformed young adult literature." *The Chocolate War* has become a classic, a staple of the high school English curriculum. Yet would-be censors, perhaps troubled by its darkness and uncompromising ending, continue to attempt to ban it on unfounded grounds of explicit sexuality and excessive profanity. In a list compiled by the American Library Association of the most frequently challenged books of the past decade [1990–2000], *The Chocolate War* is number four.

After the success of his first YA novel, Cormier astounded critics three years later with the brilliantly constructed psychological thriller *I Am the Cheese*. The story moves on three different levels that are intricately braided together, raising many questions that are not resolved until the very end when the carefully created illusion, an entire false plot, is suddenly swept away to reveal a completely unsuspected (but logically constructed) reality. In the following years, Cormier continued to surprise his readers with the originality of each new book while maintaining a continuity of recognizable style and themes that came to be called cormieresque: short cinematic scenes, taut dialogue, a deceptively straightforward story undergirded by intricate structure and layers of tricky allusion and metaphor, an intense focus on the emotion of the situation, and a dark awareness of evil as an implacable obstacle in human affairs. *After the First Death* (1979) compares the terrible naivete of a young terrorist with an army general's fa-natical patriotism in a novel shimmering with built-in puzzles and trapdoors. A volume of short stories, *Eight Plus One* (1980), was followed by the stark experimental-hospital set-ting and soaring ending of *The Bumblebee Flies Anyway* (1983); the eagerly awaited sequel *Beyond the Chocolate War* (1985) used the magician's trick of misdirection for some surprising effects and intriguing character twists. *Fade* (1988) broke new ground for Cormier with its sprawling three-part story that bordered on science fiction—the tale of a boy cursed with the hereditary ability to make himself invisible. It opens with a gentle autobiographical coming-of-age story drawn from Cormier's own French-Canadian family background, shifts into a brittle Manhattan-set examination of the nature of fic-tion and reality, and ends with a horror fantasy.

Readers had barely gotten their bearings after this unset-tling blend of truth and wild imagination when Cormier sur-prised them once again with his gentlest (and least known) novel, *Other Bells for Us to Ring* (1990), the story of eleven-year-old Darcy, who is both attracted to and terrified by the Catholicism of her friend Kathleen Mary, and who is desper-ate for a miracle to bring her father back from World War II. The story is unusual for Cormier in that its protagonist is a girl and the intended audience is middle school readers. *Tunes for Bears to Dance To* (1992) was also aimed at this younger readership, but in *We All Fall Down* (1991) and *In the Middle of the Night* (1995) Cormier returned to a more mature explo-ration of themes of guilt and salvation and love denied. Many reviewers found *Tenderness* (1997) profoundly disturbing in its ultimately sympathetic portrayal of a young serial killer, but it remains one of Cormier's most popular books with teens. *Heroes* (1998) is told by the (literally) faceless Francis Joseph Cassavant, who has returned from WWII to Cormier's fictional hometown of Monument to take revenge both on himself and his sweetheart's rapist. And Cormier once again shook up his readers' expectations with a fresh new direction in his most recent book, the autobiographical verse novel *Frenchtown Summer* (1999), told in a series of evocative and poignant short poems. A final novel, with the working title "The Rag and Bone Shop," was nearly complete at his death and [was published in 2001].

Contrast Between the Novels and the Man

The contrast between Robert Cormier's dark novels and the sunny and kindly nature of the man himself was always a revelation to fans meeting him for the first time. He lived a life of great stability and contentment, growing up in a large, warm French-Canadian and Irish-American family in the small mill town of Leominster, Massachusetts (the real-life Monument); marrying Constance Senay, the girl of his dreams; working as a newspaper man for many years and writing fiction on weekends in the midst of his noisy family of four growing children. Not until he was almost fifty did he find success as a young adult writer, with the help of his agent Marilyn Marlow. Although Cormier suffered from shyness and bullies in his own adolescence, he never deliberately set out to address these issues by writing for teens. He often said, "I've aimed for the intelligent reader and have often found that that reader is fourteen years old." His young readers were important to him, and he wrote long personal replies to the hundreds of letters he received from young fans. One of the worst-kept secrets of YA fiction has been that Cormier embedded his own phone number in *I Am the Cheese*, and young fans who discovered that fact and dared to call him up always found a sympathetic listener.

Those who knew Cormier, and even those who met him casually, were overwhelmed by his simple goodness. He cared about people, and, though he was never physically robust, he gave away his time and energy unstintingly—traveling and speaking to august literary assemblies as well as to awestruck kids in libraries and small-town school boards under censor-ship fire; giving interviews to anybody who asked, counseling new writers, and talking for hours to teens who called him on the phone. This world-renowned author spent the last spring of his life writing a history of the parish as a gift for St. Cecilia's Church, where he had been educated by nuns and had worshipped all his life.

Robert Cormier loved his young readers, and he loved his work. [In 2000] I interviewed Bob once again and asked him, "In your writing career, have you accomplished what you set out to do in the beginning?" He answered with characteristic humility: "Oh, yes. My dream was to be known as a writer and to be able to produce at least one book that would be read by people. That dream came true with the publication of my first novel—and all the rest has been a sweet bonus. All I've ever wanted to do, really, was write."

Social Issues in Literature

CHAPTER 2

The Chocolate War and Peer Pressure

The Chocolate War
Shows the Power of Peer
Pressure in High School

Joyce Moss and George Wilson

Joyce Moss and George Wilson have edited numerous reference works for young adults, including Profiles in American History *and* Peoples of the World.

According to Joyce Moss and George Wilson, The Chocolate War *is an example of realistic young-adult fiction, which had just begun to emerge as a genre in the 1960s. The novel has as its setting a private Catholic boys' school and introduces the social issues specific to private education—including the economic necessity for fund-raising initiatives such as chocolate sales. Although Jerry is defeated by the gang in the novel, Moss and Wilson say he successfully stands up to peer pressure and demonstrates the importance of individual choice.*

Although adolescent novels such as *The Chocolate War* now line the shelves of bookstores and libraries nationwide, young readers did not always have such literature at their disposal. In fact, relative to the history of the written word, the teenage novel is a new genre. During the 1930s, secondary education enrollments nearly doubled, giving rise to a new and powerful class of readers. Prior to this period, teachers and authors had, for the most part, ignored the tastes of adolescents, choosing instead to rely on the so-called "literary classics" for reading fare. While these sufficed for some chil-

Joyce Moss and George Wilson, "Overview: *The Chocolate War*," *Literature and Its Times: Profiles of 300 Notable Literary Works and the Historical Events That Influenced Them*, vol. 5: *Civil Rights Movements to Future Times (1960–2000)*, by Joyce Moss and George Wilson, Detroit: Gale, 1997, pp. 61–66. Copyright © 1997 Joyce Moss and George Wilson, Copyright © 2007 Gale. Reproduced by permission of Gale, a part of Cengage Learning.

dren, educators found that the mandatory reading of formalized literature often turned young minds away from literary experiences that they might have enjoyed later in their intellectual careers. With the burgeoning enrollments, teachers began to consider alternative methods of instruction. Researchers compiled psychological studies of adolescents and discovered that, contrary to popular opinion, older children did seek to broaden their experiences through reading. During this same time, May Lamberton Becker, an educational literature editor, compiled a survey of almost eight hundred young adults. Through their letters she found that most preferred romance and adventure tales such as *Lorna Doone, Ramona*, and *Ben Hur*. These results indicated that the adolescent reading problem stemmed not from a resistance to learning, but rather from a paucity of appealing material. Although educators debated over what types of new reading materials should be promoted, they nevertheless initiated a move toward the acceptance of popular young adult fiction.

Young Adult Lit Becomes Its Own Genre

By the 1960s, adolescent literature had matured into its own genre with three primary areas of concern: the individual and his or her growth; social problems and responsibility; and the youth's concern with world events. Librarians, authors, and educators noted that teenagers increasingly sought out books that portrayed honest visions of the world, with all of its virtues and vices. When first published in 1951, for instance, J.D. Salinger's *Catcher in the Rye* created quite a controversy for its depiction of a character in need of psychological help. The censorship debate that ensued suggested that adolescents might not have the capabilities to deal with negative portrayals of the world. By the late 1960s, however, most educators had accepted the growing teenage interest in novels that dealt honestly with personal or social problems. For example, a 1960 survey cites such political novels as *Animal Farm* and

The Ugly American as current favorites for young adults. With the mid-century spread of television, the American youth was exposed to the same mature, often violent images that the previous generation had encountered only later in life. By the late 1960s, for the first time in history the American public could view on a daily basis, through the nightly newscasts, the bloodshed occurring as a result of warfare—in this case, the war in Vietnam. Given such an environment, adolescents seemed no longer to need shielding from the harsh worlds that might await them between the covers of a novel.

Also during this era, the civil rights movement spawned a growth in minority literature. Librarians actually pleaded with editors to provide youths with books that offered realistic portrayals of ghetto life and for ones that used regional or ethnic vernacular. Robert Cormier's *The Chocolate War* aptly represents this turn to realistic fiction for youth. It does not deal with racial issues, but it does concern an individual's painful struggle to defy the status quo. Like other popular novels of its day, Cormier's book paints a realistic image of the sometimes harsh world in which adolescents live.

Private Schools vs. Public Schools

The private, all-male school of the novel differs vastly from the typical public institution. While the classes offered at the novel's Trinity High School certainly compare to the curricula of public schools, its social atmosphere is entirely unique. In addition to its single-sex composition, Trinity's Catholic affiliation sets it markedly apart from public high schools. The fictional school does, however, resemble many other private religious schools of modern times.

A 58 percent majority of Catholic schools are located in cities. With enrollments much smaller than in public institutions, private schools offer more compact classes with lower student-to-teacher ratios. In the 1970s, the average enrollment for Catholic high schools was about five hundred. By contrast, many urban public schools boasted student bodies of several thousand. In many cases minority enrollment was low, so the composition of these schools was generally homogeneous.

Trinity is a fictional Catholic day school catering to the children of local blue- and white-collar workers. In real life, wealthier families have tended to send their children instead to prep (preparatory) schools that board them away from home. At the other end of the spectrum, the poorer families of the community are unable to afford even Catholic day school tuition. The ability to pay tuition, however, is not the only challenge to enrollment. As private entities, Catholic schools can refuse admission to applicants for a variety of reasons. Typically the administration relies on school records, achievement test scores, and personal references when deciding whether or not to accept a prospective student. These rigorous standards do not relax once a student enters the school.

Catholic high schools emphasize college preparation in setting academic goals. While the schools offer such typical core classes as physics, mathematics, and foreign languages, they also provide students with opportunities in independent study and off-campus college courses. Naturally schools also insist on a schedule of religious classes as a graduation requirement. Students need not practice Catholicism to attend Catholic schools, but the majority do.

A concern of the first order for private schools is, of course, their own survival. Although current statistics indicate that America's 20,000 private schools account for 10 percent of the secondary education sector, enrollments in Catholic schools are on the decline. This translates into significant monetary losses for these institutions. In Cormier's novel, Brother Leon expresses concern over the financial future of Trinity. With enrollments down, the annual chocolate sale serves an important role in augmenting the school's income. As Trinity earns a percentage of every chocolate sold, the success or failure of the sale directly impacts the budget of the

Students adjust magnification on their microscopes during biology class at St. Stithians College, an integrated Methodist school in Johannesburg, South Africa, circa 1990. © Gideon Mendel/Corbis.

high school. A student refusing participation in the sale would appear to have little or no concern for the welfare of the school in general. For this reason, Jerry's rejection of the sale is not viewed as an individual decision. By refusing to work with his classmates for the welfare of the school, he appears indifferent to the future of Trinity altogether. At a public school funded by tax dollars, this issue would take on less significance. Trinity, however, is a private Catholic school that demands loyalty from the students that it instructs. In the novel Jerry is ostracized, which certainly does not reflect the kindest of Christian values. It does, however, reflect the reality of financial hardship, when in some cases hard-line capitalism often defeats the "love thy neighbor" principle.

Athletics Play a Central Role

Far from being a mere sport, football plays a consequential role in Jerry Renault's life at Trinity. While trying out for the freshman team, he suffers humiliation from his coach as well as physical abuse from older players. He nonetheless competes for a spot on the roster. By the novel's close, the sport ironically forms a safe haven for Jerry. Ostracized by the entire campus for his lack of participation in the chocolate sale, the freshman turns to football as a measure of normalcy in his suddenly confounded life. Jerry, like many other high school athletes, embraces sports as an integral core of the educational experience.

Across the United States, communities share similar enthusiasm for the high school competitions of their local athletes. The American obsession with sports has as much to do with the principles taught through games as it does with the game at hand. In one comprehensive survey, three out of five respondents agreed that athletes provide the best overall role models for children. Through sports, adolescents can learn many of the social values necessary for success in work and other aspects of life. They come to understand fair play, respect for authority, and good sportsmanship. Last, but certainly not least, they realize the thrill of victory. All this emphasis on athletics has spawned such telltale American slogans as "winning isn't everything, it is the only thing." and "A tie is like kissing your sister." Fostered in schools, the competitive drive, many believe, serves adolescents well not only in teaching them these principles but also in generating school spirit.

Played during the fall season, football kicks off the school year, so to speak. In fact, the sport provides an overall example of the educational institutionalization of athletics. At the turn of the century [i.e., 1900], football was an incredibly hazardous sport with many injuries and deaths reported annually. Although some schools sought out coaches, faculties originally resisted this move. They feared any type of official association between the school and such an "abusive" sport. The institutionalization of football, however, solved these problems. With adults rather than students leading the field practice and play, rules were adhered to, training facilities were improved, and injuries declined. In 1919 the National Education Association issued a report entitled "The Cardinal Principles of Secondary Education," which extolled the virtues of organized school athletics. By 1932 sociologist Willard Waller had concluded that "Of all activities, athletics is the chief. . . . It is the most flourishing and the most revered culture pattern." Within a relatively short time, organized athletics had proved their importance in the educational arena.

Jerry Is Ostracized, Then Beaten

When Jerry Renault begins his freshman year at Trinity, the local all-boys Catholic day school, he does not intend to earn an infamous reputation. Still recovering from the recent death of his mother, Jerry wants only to lead a normal high school life. He and his father are not very close, and so Jerry's life has been quite lonely for the past year. Within the first week of school, Jerry earns a position on the football team and seems poised to begin a successful freshman year. However, Archie Costello, the leader of a secret society known as the Vigils, has other plans for Jerry.

The Vigils, through their underground student body network, run the social order at Trinity. Every few months or so, Archie and his cohorts choose various students to burden with Assignments. They summon their victims to secluded Vigil meetings, where Archie hands down a sentence. Those chosen cannot refuse their tasks, nor can they tell anyone about their activities when they execute them. In one session, for instance, Archie commands a new freshman to loosen all the furniture screws in a classroom. The following day, mayhem ensues as the class literally falls to pieces. No one dares to defy the Vigil Assignments, as the students fear the wrath of the society. Unfortunately for Jerry, he catches Archie's eye one afternoon at football practice. The Vigil leader singles him out for an Assignment, and orders Jerry to refuse participation in the school chocolate sale.

Each year, Trinity sponsors a schoolwide sale of chocolate candy. A private institution, Trinity relies solely on tuition income to fund its facilities. The proceeds from the annual sale serve as a necessary supplement to the school budget. This year, however, the sale brings with it an added anxiety. With the principal of the school temporarily hospitalized, one of the other teachers, Brother Leon, has taken over the administrative duties at Trinity. Unbeknownst to the other faculty members, Leon signs for twice the normal amount of chocolates. The monk quickly panics over his fiscal risk and, in his desperation, enlists the aid of the Vigils. Recognizing the opportunity to join forces with a faculty member, Archie quickly agrees. The arrangement signifies an unprecedented alliance between the Vigils and the administration of Trinity.

Although the Assignment only mandates that Jerry refuse to sell the chocolates for ten days, he extends the sentence of his own accord. Inspired by a poster that asks, "Do I dare disturb the universe?" Jerry decides to keep refusing to participate in the sale. At first, Jerry's refusal to sell causes only minor tensions at the school. Some of the students even support his independent stance. When chocolate sales fall well behind statistics of years past, however, Brother Leon and the Vigils single out Jerry as a symbol of insolence. The monk puts pressure on the Vigils to pick up the pace of the sales, and the Vigils, in turn, transfer this pressure onto Jerry. They begin to torment him by making prank calls to his house, vandalizing his locker, and beating him up. Nevertheless, Jerry refuses to submit. Angered by the freshman's defiance, Archie rallies his group to sell chocolates like never before. In this manner, they hope to humiliate Jerry for his audacity in challenging the Vigils. As chocolate sales escalate, the school turns on Jerry, accusing him of apathy and disregard for the welfare of the school. Jerry ironically finds himself ostracized for carrying out an "assignment" that he originally undertook for fear of not fitting in.

Eventually the chocolate sale ends with Brother Leon and Trinity successfully meeting the school quota. Still the Vigils refuse to relax in their pursuit of Jerry. They arrange for an after-school fight at which spectators both choreograph and bet on the physical blows that Jerry must endure. Brother Leon appears as an invited guest to watch the event. Jerry suffers such harm that an ambulance must be called to take him away. Although he loses the physical bout, he maintains his dignity in becoming the first student to defy the school, the Vigils, and his educational universe in general.

Jerry Defies Peer Pressure

A turning point in Jerry's life occurs one afternoon as he waits for his bus following football practice. Standing at the stop in his school uniform and tie, he stares at a group of hippies across the street. One man confronts him, asking, "Hey, man, you think we're in a zoo? That why you stare?" Unable to respond, Jerry boards the bus. The man continues stating, "Square boy. Middle-aged at fourteen, fifteen. Already caught in a routine. . . . You're missing a lot of things in the world, better not miss the bus." For some reason unknown to Jerry at the time, the event haunts him. He questions his own blind acceptance of peer pressure and authority. Later in the novel, Jerry recalls the hippie as he stares at a poster lining his locker. The picture shows a lone figure on a stretch of beach with the caption "Do I dare disturb the universe?" Although he had never done so before, Jerry decides to answer in the affirmative by the way he acts in regard to the chocolate sale.

By refusing to sell Trinity's chocolate, Jerry not only defies his teachers, but he also counters the wishes of the school's "in crowd." In fact, he alienates himself from his own peer group. In the world of a modern-day teenager, this type of self-imposed separation is not easy to endure. As part of a group separated from other generations, typical teens spend the majority of their time with their own peer group and learn to conform to it. This is especially true in private schools like Trinity. With their familiar environments being class-rooms, shopping malls, playing fields, and automobiles, ado-lescents virtually invent their own society. This, in turn, places a great deal of importance on the judgment of one's peers. With few other influences that matter as much to them at this point in their lives, teens look to one another for social ap-proval.

In the novel, the Vigils virtually run the school—and, as often the case, a natural leader has emerged. Teenage "in" groups tend to gravitate toward leaders who possess good per-sonality, nice hair, good grooming, fine clothes, and money. Mentioned far less frequently as a factor among teens is aca-demic success. As the novel opens, Jerry hopes to attain these symbols of popularity, but he loses his enthusiasm for group acceptance by the book's close. Perhaps the hippie, a symbol of the counterculture movement, inspires him. Or perhaps Jerry reaches this state of independence because he was forced to grow up quickly after the death of his mother. The novel remains ambiguous as to the impetus for the young man's de-fiant stance. Even Jerry himself cannot say why he does what he does, and in the end, even he questions the intelligence of his choice. For whatever reason, however, Jerry does opt to go against the grain. In doing so, he becomes a target for those who govern the social structure.

Emphasizing Individual Choice

The Chocolate War emphasizes self-reliance and self-respect of the individual. Because of his decision, Jerry must learn to survive alone within his society of peers. Much of Cormier's interest in individual independence comes from his own expe-rience. While still a young boy, Cormier lost his father to can-cer. Like Jerry in the novel, the author matured through ado-lescence in a single-parent household. Later in life, his son refused participation in a school candy sale. Although the boy did not undergo the extreme harassment that Jerry suffers, his actions nonetheless inspired the elder Cormier to develop the defiance into a novel.

While many critics found the novel disturbing for its "distorted view of reality and . . . feeling of absolute hopelessness," others praised the work for its stark realism. One critic opined that "Robert Cormier does not leave his readers without hope, but he does deliver a warning: they may not plead innocence, ignorance, or prior commitments when the threat of tyranny confronts them." Clearly a dichotomous opinion of the book exists. In spite of or perhaps because of this critical debate, *The Chocolate War* is now considered by many to be one of the more important adolescent novels of modern times.

The *Chocolate War* Incites Readers to Activism

Sylvia Patterson Iskander

Sylvia Patterson Iskander is professor emerita of literature at the University of Louisiana–Lafayette.

In the following selection, Sylvia Patterson Iskander claims that critics have erroneously faulted Robert Cormier for presenting a vision of hopelessness. She believes they are misreading the levels of irony in the novel that teenagers relate to and understand. There are five different ways of reading a text to help understand it, she says. Among these are the real world, the social and cultural world, and the literary world. Cormier himself believes that his novels argue for individual responsibility, not for a pessimistic view of life.

The young-adult novels of Robert Cormier—*The Chocolate War, I Am the Cheese, After the First Death, The Bumblebee Flies Anyway,* and *Beyond the Chocolate War*—have been criticized for the bleak, hopeless world they describe. Norma Bagnall says of *The Chocolate War,* "Hopelessness pervades the entire story"; "there are no adults worth emulating"; "only the ugly is presented through the novel's language, action and imagery." Anne Scott MacLeod describes Cormier's work as "a world of painful harshness, where choices are few and consequences desperate." . . .

Criticized for Pessimism

Some of these comments have been answered in an article by Betty Carter and Karen Harris, who argue that "Cormier does not leave his readers without hope, but he does deliver a

Sylvia Patterson Iskander, "Readers, Realism, and Robert Cormier," *Children's Literature: Annual of the Modern Language Association Division on Children's Literature and the Children's Literature Association,* vol. 15, 1987, pp. 7–18. Reproduced by permission.

warning: they may not plead innocence, ignorance, or prior commitments when the threat of tyranny confronts them." Yet the objections point accurately to problems raised by these novels. The almost universal distress about Cormier's work springs directly from the power and consistency of his imagined world, which convinces readers that it bears a recognizable relationship to the "real world" and yet appears to leave no room for anything but pessimism about the survival of Cormier's protagonists. Because of this, several school boards and parental groups in New York, Massachusetts, South Carolina, and Arizona have tried to ban Cormier's novels from the classroom.

Agreement between author and audience is not always possible for readers of Cormier's novels. The conventions of the genre of the young-adult novel, according to MacLeod, may deal with harshness and stern reality, but they must offer some hope, "some affirmative message." She among others does not find any affirmation of the traditional adolescent "themes of adjustment, acceptance, and understanding" in any of Cormier's novels. She feels, for example, that when Jerry, the protagonist of *The Chocolate War*, is carried off the football field on a stretcher, Cormier "has abandoned an enduring American myth to confront his teenaged readers with life as it more often is—with the dangers of dissent, the ferocity of systems as they protect themselves, the power of the pressure to conform." She correctly states that the "discussion of political evil [in *I Am the Cheese*] is cast in fiercely contemporary terms" and that Artkin, Miro, and the general in *After the First Death* "disavow their humanity in the same moment that they seal their innocence by choosing never to question nor even to contemplate questioning." MacLeod does not, however, mention either Ben Marchand or Kate Forrester, who are positive role models in *After the First Death*. She comments on Cormier's powerful ability to reach the innermost thoughts of his readers and to make them question the contemporary systems within which they find themselves, but she does not explore this subject.

There are, it seems to me, three aspects of this problem. First, who is Cormier's reader, or what are some of the characteristics of young-adult readers? Teenagers stand at a threshold; not fully committed to the adult world, they are uncertain of their own strength, yet they clearly tend toward moral idealism. Second, what do adults consider appropriate reading for adolescents? Many parents and critics feel strongly that literature for teenagers at this vulnerable period in their lives should help them develop their sense of moral choice and responsibility by presenting clear-cut guidelines. Finally, what does Cormier require of his readers? The answer to this question touches on the concerns raised by the other questions, for, rather than asking his readers to endorse simple affirmations, Cormier demands that they respond to ironies and qualifications.

The reader—parent, school board member, or young adult—who rejects a Cormier novel as totally without hope has failed to recognize its positive elements because these are presented ironically and indirectly. The successful reader must recognize the various levels of reality present in these novels and extrapolate beyond the novel's close to see an extended moral development. . . .

Parents may justifiably ask how many teenagers are capable of so perceptive a reading, and yet adults often underestimate the teenage reader, who may understand the thrust of a Cormier novel in a practical rather than critical fashion. Some of the arguments between parents and children about the books have shown teenagers applying the received meaning of the book to constructive action in their own world. For example, consider the key passage in *The Chocolate War* where Brother Leon, the corrupt headmaster of Trinity High School, deliberately intimidates young Gregory Bailey, while waiting for some protest from Bailey's classmates, who know that he is innocent. When one voice finally protests, "Aw, let the kid alone," Brother Leon says it is "a feeble protest, too little and too late." Brother Leon teaches about the dehumanization of the Nazis by practicing it; he shows that this moral corruption occurred at least in part because there was not enough resistance to tyranny. Although Leon's motives are not entirely altruistic, the perceptive reader recognizes the author's message. When the protagonist of *The Chocolate War*, Jerry Renault, lies on the football field at the novel's close, crushed both physically and emotionally, the novel dramatizes the lesson and carries it to its conclusion. Who helped Jerry? Who resisted tyranny? No one. For nearly two hundred pages Jerry is a hero; in the final four pages he is defeated, at least for the present. In Cormier's sequel, *Beyond the Chocolate War*, Jerry returns to Monument after a lengthy recovery in Canada. He gradually regains his physical and mental strength until he is able to face, deflate, and defeat Emile Janza, his tormentor in the earlier novel. This might lead us to consider the two books as an extended version of the American myth of the victorious nonconformist in which a youngster surmounts physical and emotional obstacles to achieve a triumph that is more than just an athletic victory. The outcome of *The Chocolate War* must, however, be considered on its own merits, and it contains an apparent rejection of this myth. The question must be asked: does Jerry's crushing defeat leave the reader hopeless?

Five Levels to Cormier Novels

When their parents objected to the teaching of *The Chocolate War*, the students in a New York school petitioned to keep the book. In answer to one student who suggested that the signing of the petition be unanimous, a thirteen-year-old boy said no one should be compelled, as Jerry was, to join the majority. From the boy's statement the parents realized that the novel had provided an ethical example to their children; they voted to keep the book.

Why did this boy understand the message of the book when others, including adults, failed? The answer, I believe, lies in his ability to perceive the different levels of meaning or "reality" in these texts. The complexity of Cormier's work challenges our notions of the proper relationship between events and their meanings. Tzvetan Todorov explains that "reality" or "verisimilitude" may be "the relation of a particular text to another general and diffuse text which might be called 'public opinion,'" "whatever tradition makes suitable or expected in a particular genre," or "the mask which conceals the text's own laws and which we are supposed to take for a relation with reality."

Jonathan Culler takes Todorov's three definitions of verisimilitude or *vraisemblance* a step further and distinguishes "five ways in which a text may be brought into contact with and defined in relation to another text which helps to make it intelligible."

> First, there is the socially given text, that which is taken as the "real world." Second, but in some cases difficult to distinguish from the first, is a general cultural text: shared knowledge which would be recognized by participants as part of the culture and hence subject to corruption or modification but which none the less serves as a kind of "nature." Third, there are the texts or conventions of a genre, a specifically literary and artificial *vraisemblance*. Fourth comes what might be called the natural attitude to the artificial, where the text explicitly cites and exposes *vraisemblance* of the third kind so as to reinforce its own authority. And finally, there is the complex *vraisemblance* of specific intertextualities, where one work takes another as its basis or point of departure and must be assimilated in relation to it.

The reader of a Cormier novel will experience no difficulty with the first level, the representation of the socially given world. The novels all appear to derive from a contemporary world, with a stress on its unpleasant aspects, such as corruption in a Catholic school (*Chocolate War*), the murder and torture of innocents (*I Am the Cheese* and *After the First*

Death), suicide (*After the First Death* and *Beyond the Chocolate War*), or teenagers who are terminally ill (*Bumblebee*). Cormier sets all his novels in a fictional Monument, Massachusetts, whose details, typical of small-town American life, reinforce the sense of relationship to the social world of his readers. (Monument also illustrates Culler's fifth level of vraisemblance, since these intertextual repetitions appear to offer external confirmation of the world that lies behind each novel.)

Similarly, Cormier's characters are plausible in the context of our social experience and expectations. Certainly the terrorists in *After the First Death* seem to fit a stereotypical portrait of terrorists; they believe that their cause is more important than human life. The teenagers in all the novels act like teenagers; for instance, Amy and Adam from *I Am the Cheese* are young adults and yet they pull off "numbers" or pranks in grocery stores and parking lots. Jerry Renault of *The Chocolate War* is atypical, however, in his total nonconformity, but even such an unusual teenager appeals to the young adult's sense of uncertain identity and therefore seems valid and believable as a role model.

The second, cultural level of vraisemblance also presents only minor problems of recognition to the reader. The notions of innocence, betrayal, sacrifice, terrorism, death, love, and fear are intelligible as appropriate motives or products of actions and situations, given our cultural codes. At this level, Cormier's characters engage systems of values that readers can accept as plausible, whether or not they actually coincide with our own beliefs; however, it might be argued that Cormier violates our generally hopeful vision of the world by concentrating almost exclusively on the bleaker aspects of life.

Controversial Triumph of the Protagonist

Yet the third, generic level of vraisemblance will cause more adult readers to experience their first difficulty with Cormier's texts. At this level, literary norms govern the author's imaginative world. Two of the principal norms governing the structure of literature for children and adolescents are the identification of the protagonist with morality and the triumph of good over evil—in other words, a victorious protagonist. Hope in the novels of Cormier is both reinforced and shattered on this level. In *The Chocolate War*, Jerry Renault draws our moral admiration because he defies corruption and pressure from three sources, thus maintaining his individuality. He refuses to surrender to an inner desire to conform. He refuses to yield to peer pressure whether it be from the gang that tries to manipulate him or from his friend Goober, who worries about Jerry's nonconformity. And he refuses to submit to the tyranny of Brother Leon. Through this nonconformism, then, Cormier offers the reader a strong moral model that paradoxically conforms to narrative convention but does not meet our expectations in that good does not triumph over evil.

The structure of Cormier's plot, instead, shatters our expectations. Powerful American stereotypes insist that the good nonconformist must, in fiction, win at least a qualified victory. Cormier's testing of Jerry seems to prepare the way for a conventional reversal; readers anticipate a stunning last-minute victory by the hero. But when the hero is crushed and brutally beaten, his very survival in question, many readers feel betrayed and disoriented. The overthrow of the nonconformist protagonist at the close, like the killing of Kate in *After the First Death*, violates the anticipated outcome of the action; within the myth, the validation of nonconformity is victory. When readers complain about Cormier's hopeless pessimism, they mean that the novel's close defies their expectations. It is this deviation from narrative convention that repels some readers, who then protest at school board meetings or forbid their children to read Cormier's books. They prefer censorship to an examination of the social issues at stake in Cormier's novels or a reappraisal of American myths.

Yet Cormier deliberately violates our optimistic expectations in a strategy designed to convert the reader from a passive to an active role. He carefully develops, for example, the positive aspects of Jerry's home life, which was warm and loving before his mother's death and which can be so again when Mr. Renault recovers from his grief over his wife's death. In Jerry's "good" home he learned his values and developed the courage to fight back. Jerry's supportive friendship with Goober demonstrates the need of an individual to choose his friends, and it contrasts with the manipulation of an individual by the gang. Although Goober through human weakness fails Jerry, his guilt and anguish over his failure to help offer positive reinforcement to the adolescent reader who is struggling with his own problems of loyalty and betrayal. Although the novel does not resolve the social problems it raises, it does show how we can gain the moral strength to face them. Thus if—and it is a large if—one accepts the notion of a vital link between response to reading and behavior in the "real world," true hopelessness will result only if the reader concludes that people should not fight for their beliefs.

Cormier ironically calls upon our expectation that the author will finally reestablish moral order, and thus he employs Culler's fourth kind of realism. He forcibly reminds us that the reader cannot count on fictional escapes from the hard choices of life. The same message is evident to the receptive reader of *Beyond the Chocolate War.* Evil surrounds us and will continue to do so; when an Archie Costello graduates, a Bunting is waiting to take his place. Archie articulates Cormier's message clearly: "'Know what, Obie? You could have said *no* anytime, anytime at all [to joining the gang, to finding victims for them]. But you didn't.'" Obie's reaction dramatically reinforces Cormier's point: "A sound escaped from Obie's lips, the sound a child might make hearing that his mother and father had been killed in an auto accident on their way home. The sound had death in it. And truth. The terrible truth that Archie was right, of course. He had blamed Archie all along." Obie now understands that he should have taken a stand, that we have free choice; however, his first stand—an attempt to murder Archie to rid Trinity High of him forever—shocks the reader as it shocks Obie. Fortunately Obie's plan does not succeed, but Cormier succeeds in making his audience reevaluate the individual's response to evil and those who promote it in a way that overt moralizing would never do. He forces the readers into Culler's fourth and fifth levels of realism: those who have read *The Chocolate War* with its destruction of the American myth of the victorious nonconformist will no longer take for granted the myth's validity in the sequel. Even though the sequel reestablishes the myth, we no longer approach a Cormier novel with the same expectations that we have for other young-adult novels....

Cormier Teaches Personal Responsibility

Cormier relies ... on situational irony rather than verbal irony in his five young-adult novels. He forces us to contemplate such subjects as the death of innocent hostages, diseased teenagers, and civic-minded citizens, the defeat of the nonconformist, the suicide of several boys betrayed—all for the purpose of making the reader move beyond the close of the novels to a new sense of personal responsibility. For the reader, unlike the characters, has a second chance. From the defeat of the protagonists who struggle for right in an evil, corrupt, and convincingly real world, where no law of poetic justice prevails, can come the wisdom and understanding of the next generation of individuals who will fight tyranny, who will stand up for their principles, who will be the heroes trying to make the world a better place. Gregory Bailey's classmates learn that Nazism took hold because not enough people protested; Barney tells Billy the Kidney that the bad thing is not doing anything; Obie realizes he has a choice. Mr. Farmer, Ben, and Kate all took positive action. That some of these failed is more realistic than the myth that people courageous enough to stand up for their beliefs will automatically be victorious.

Cormier makes his readers think long after they have closed his novels because he chooses not to follow the literary norm of the happy ending. The climactic structure of his novels with their shocking, unhappy, but quite realistic endings reinforces not the temporary defeats or a bleak pessimism, but rather a longing for justice. His books "argue" for moral responsibility far more effectively than sermonizing or stereotypical formulas of virtue automatically triumphant. Cormier himself said in a letter to me, "[The] message that I have always felt was implicit in the novels, [is] that evil only occurs when we allow it to occur, it does not blossom by itself." Hope for the future is in the minds of Cormier's more astute teenage readers as they recognize that in the "real world" as well as the literary world they themselves are the next generation heroes.

The Chocolate War Is About Taking a Stand Against Evil

Patty Campbell

Patty Campbell is considered Robert Cormier's major biographer.

In the following selection, Patty Campbell contends that The Chocolate War *is about the nature of evil in the world. Three of the characters in the book—Brother Leon, Archie, and Emile—all represent different forms of evil. On another level, Campbell asserts that the book can be read as a study of tyranny. No one speaks up for Jerry; if just one person had had the courage to challenge Leon and the Vigils, others might have joined in. Ultimately, she concludes, it is not about winning or losing but taking a stand.*

*T*he Chocolate War] works superbly as a tragic yarn, an exciting piece of storytelling. Many young adults, especially younger readers, will simply want to enjoy it at this level, and Cormier himself would be the first to say that there is nothing wrong with that. A work of literature should be first of all a good story. But a work of literature also has resonance, richness, a broader intent than just the fate of the characters. For the reader who wants to dig a bit beneath the surface, there is a wealth of hidden meaning and emotion in *The Chocolate War*. How does Cormier achieve this atmosphere of dark, brooding inevitability? What are the overarching themes from which the events of the plot are hung? And, most of all, just what is the crucial thing that he is trying to tell us?

A Cinematic Technique

A look at Cormier's style in this book will show first of all the driving, staccato rhythms. The sentences are short and punchy,

Patricia J. Campbell, *"The Chocolate War," Presenting Robert Cormier*, Boston: Twayne Publishers, 1985, pp. 34–44.

and the chapters are often no more than two pages. He uses dialogue to move the action quickly forward and to establish character and situation in brief, broad strokes. His technique is essentially cinematic; if he wants to make a psychological or philosophical point he does so visually with a symbolic event or an interchange between characters, rather than reflecting in a verbal aside. Tension is built by an escalating chain of events, each a little drama of its own. "Rather than waiting for one big climax, I try to create a lot of little conflicts," he explains. "A series of explosions as I go along."

The point of view snaps back and forth from boy to boy in succeeding chapters, a more focused use of the technique called "omniscient observer." First we see Archie through Obie's eyes, then we are inside Jerry's head, then we watch Leon and The Goober squirm under Archie's gaze, then we are looking up at him from Emile's dwarfish mind, then we watch Brother Leon's classroom performance through Jerk's quiet presence, and so on. The variety of perspectives develops our understanding of the characters and reveals the complex interweaving of motivations and dependencies. The shift is unobtrusive but can be easily detected by a close look at the text. Less subtly, there are occasional tags that clue the reader to a change in voice: Brian Cochran and Obie, for instance, are inclined to think, "For crying out loud!" while Archie, among others, is addicted to the ironic use of the word *beautiful*. Cormier is too fine a writer, of course, to descend to imitation slang in order to indicate that this is a teenager speaking. Nothing dates a book more quickly than trendiness, as he learned from "The Rumple Country," and his understanding of the quality of adolescence goes far deeper than picking up the latest expression.

Much has been made of Cormier's imagery, and many essays and articles have been written on his metaphors and similes, his allusions and personifications. Sometimes it seems that Cormier is merely exercising his virtuosity for the reader:

"his voice curled into a question mark," or "he poured himself liquid through the sunrise streets." But most of the time his metaphors are precisely calculated to carry the weight of the emotion he is projecting. Carter, about to tackle Jerry, looks "like some monstrous reptile in his helmet." Leon, thwarted, has "a smile like the kind an undertaker fixes on the face of a corpse." Jerry, happy, scuffles through "crazy cornflake leaves" but, sad, sees autumn leaves flutter down "like doomed and crippled birds." Jerry's father, preparing their loveless dinner, slides a casserole "into the oven like a letter into a mailbox." Sometimes the imagery is vividly unpleasant, as some reviewers have complained, but it is always appropriate to the intensity of the thing that Cormier is trying to say. There is a whole bouquet of bad smells in *The Chocolate War*, starting with Brother Leon's rancid bacon breath. The evening comes on as "the sun bleeding low in the sky and spurting its veins." Sweat moves like small moist bugs on Jerry's forehead. The vanquished Rollo's vomiting sounds like a toilet flushing.

Literary and Biblical Allusions

Literary and biblical allusions, too, enrich the alert reader's experience of the novel. Shakespeare, the Bible, and the poetry of T.S. Eliot are the most obvious sources. "Cut me, do I not bleed?" thinks Emile, like Shylock [from Shakespeare's *The Merchant of Venice*]. For Jerry, like Saint Peter, a thousand cocks have crowed. The quotation on the poster in his locker is from Eliot's "The Love Song of J. Alfred Prufrock." One reviewer has gone so far as to write an essay drawing parallels between Jerry and [Shakespeare's] Hamlet, Archie and [Shakespeare's villain in *Othello*,] Iago. Cormier denies building in this particular analogy, but admits that such references may come from his subconscious. The sophisticated reader, too, can absorb them subliminally, without conscious analysis.

Many of these allusions are not isolated flourishes, but fit together into larger structures of meaning. As one example, the Christian symbolism in *The Chocolate War* is an indication of the importance of the book's theme to Cormier. . . . Cormier [uses] Christian symbolism to show the cosmic implications of the events he is relating. When Jerry refuses to sell the chocolates, the language suggests the Book of Revelation: "Cities fell. Earth opened. Planets tilted. Stars plummeted." In the first chapter, the goal posts remind Obie of empty crucifixes, and in the last chapter, after Jerry's martyrdom, they again remind him of—what? In his graceless state, he can't remember. When Jerry is challenged to action by the hippie, the man looks at him from across a Volkswagen so that Jerry sees only the disembodied head. The image is John the Baptist, he who was beheaded by Herod after he cried in the wilderness to announce the coming of Christ. Archie's name has myriad meanings from its root of "arch": "principal or chief," "cleverly sly and alert," "most fully embodying the qualities of its kind"; but most significantly, the reference is to the Archangel, he who fell from Heaven to be the Fallen Angel, or Lucifer himself. The Vigils, although Cormier admits only to a connotation of "vigilantes," resonate with religious meaning. The candles placed before the altar in supplication are vigil candles, and a vigil is a watch on the night preceding a religious holiday. The members of the gang stand before Archie, who basks in their admiration like a religious statue before a bank of candles. But most important, the understanding of the ultimate opposing forces of good and evil in *The Chocolate War* is a deeply Christian, or perhaps even a deeply Catholic, vision.

How does the theme of this book fit into Cormier's fascination for the nature of human confrontation with the Implacable? Each of the three villains is vulnerable, and if they cannot quite be placated, they can at least be manipulated. They are quick to see each other's weaknesses, and quick to take advantage of them for more secure positions of power. Leon has put himself in a shaky place by his overreaching ambition, and Archie sees him "riddled with cracks and crevices—running scared—open to invasion." Archie fears Leon's power over him as his teacher, and his domination of the Vigils is dependent on thinking up ever more imaginative assignments. And then there is the black box—a nemesis over which he has no control. Emile's weakness is his stupidity; he is easily conned by Archie into believing in the imaginary photograph. So none of the three is an implacable, unconquerable force; all are subject to fears and weaknesses.

Jerry Is Fighting Evil

Why then does Jerry's lone refusal seem so very doomed from the beginning? Why does the contest seem so unequal; why does the action move so inevitably toward tragedy? The answer lies in the nature of what it is he is saying "no" to. What he is opposing is not Brother Leon, not Archie, not Emile, but the monstrous force that moves them, of which they are but imperfect human agents. The Goober gives it a name: "'There's something rotten in that school. More than rotten.' He groped for the word and found it but didn't want to use it. The word didn't fit the surroundings, the sun and the bright October afternoon. It was a midnight word, a howling wind word." The word is *Evil*.

The unholy trinity of Trinity are studies in the human forms of evil. Brother Leon, who as a priest is supposedly an agent of the Divine, has sold his soul for power, even down to his exultation in the small nasty tyrannies of the classroom. Cormier has said that he chose the name Leon, a bland, soft name, to match the brother's superficial blandness. "And so is evil bland in its many disguises," he adds. Leon's appearance is deceptive: "On the surface, he was one of those pale, ingratiating kind of men who tiptoed through life on small, quick feet." "In the classroom Leon was another person altogether. Smirking, sarcastic. His thin, high voice venomous. He could hold your attention like a cobra. Instead of fangs, he used his teacher's pointer, flicking out here, there, everywhere." Leon's skin is pale, damp, and his moist eyes are like boiled onions or specimens in laboratory test tubes. When he blackmails Caroni into revealing Jerry's motivation, his fingers holding the chalk are like "the legs of pale spiders with a victim in their clutch." After he has demolished the boy, the chalk lies broken, "abandoned on the desk, like white bones, dead men's bones." The image that gradually accumulates around Leon is that of a hideous, colorless insect, a poisonous insect, crawling damp from its hiding place under a rock. Or perhaps he has emerged from even deeper underground, as Jerry suspects when he sees "a glimpse into the hell that was burning inside the teacher."

Archie is far subtler and will ultimately, when he is an adult, be more dangerous, because he is not in bondage to ambition. True, he revels in the captive audience of the Vigils, but he is not really part of that or any political structure. "I am Archie" he gloats, Archie alone. For him, the pleasure is in building intricate evil structures for their own sake. "Beautiful!" he cries as Brother Eugene falls apart like the furniture in his room, as Leon squirms under the pressure of Jerry's refusal, as Jerry struggles ever deeper into the exitless trap Archie has made for him. Yet, Archie, too, is in hell, the hell of understanding only the dark side of human nature. "People are two things," he tells Carter. "Greedy and cruel." From this knowledge comes his strength, his ability to make anybody do anything. But it is bottomless emptiness. "Life is shit," he says without emotion.

Emile Has Surrendered to Evil

Emile is the purest embodiment of evil. In him we see the horror of evil's essential quality: silliness. Emile loves to "reach" people. He giggles when he leaves a mess in the public toilet, when he gives an already-tackled football player a secret extra jab, when he loudly accuses a shy kid of farting on a crowded bus. Essentially evil is pointless. Purpose and struc-

Evil often expresses itself in human form, such as the bullying of a smaller student by a larger. Image copyright © Lisa F. Young, 2009. Used under license from Shutterstock .com.

ture belong to goodness; evil can only turn back on itself in chaos. Archie and Leon have clothed their evil with intelligence and worldly power, but Emile's surrender to darkness is revealed in all its terrible nakedness. The others recognize his non-humanity quite clearly. "An animal," they call him.

Archie is amused by Emile's simplicity but also chilled by the recognition of a kinship he is not willing to acknowledge. Emile, however, in his perverse innocence, easily sees that he and Archie are "birds of a feather," and that their differences are only a matter of intelligence. An even more terrible innocence is that of the children whom Emile recruits to ambush Jerry. "Animals," he calls them in turn, and they emerge crouching from the bushes to do his bidding like the twittering hordes of little devils in a painting by Hieronymous Bosch.

Both Archie and Emile have cross-wired their sexual energies into sadism. Emile wishes he could tell Archie how he sometimes feels "horny" when he does a particularly vicious thing. The sources of Archie's most maliciously creative ideas are found in his sexual energy, as Cormier made clear in a chapter that was never printed. In these deleted pages Archie, backed into a corner by thinking of Jerry's recalcitrance, attempts to masturbate, but his powerlessness against the situation renders him impotent. Finally he gets the glimmering of an idea—and an erection—and conceives the scheme for the boxing match that will destroy Jerry at the same moment that he achieves his climax. The chapter is stunning in its sensuality, but Cormier, on the advice of his agent and because he found he was reluctant to allow his own daughter to read it, removed it from the final manuscript.

All three villains are completely devoid of any sense of guilt. Indeed, Archie often congratulates himself on his compassion. Brother Leon is all surface; his soul is hollow, and he is the one character whose interior monologue we never hear. Repentance is totally foreign to him. Emile is even a bit defensive at being defined as a bad guy. "All right, so he liked to screw around a little, get under people's skin. That was human nature, wasn't it? A guy had to protect himself at all times. Get them before they get you. Keep people guessing—and afraid."

In chapter 4 Brother Leon mentions that Archie's father "operates an insurance business." This one shred of information is all we know about Archie's background. What could the home life of such a monster be? For that matter, what parent could live with Emile? Does Brother Leon have an aged mother somewhere? What were they all like as children? The questions are intriguing but pointless. Cormier deliberately gives us no hint of the origins of their devotion to darkness. "People can't say Archie did this because he was a deprived child or he was a victim of child abuse. I wanted him judged solely on his actions." To understand is to forgive, and to forgive real evil is to make alliance with it. To render these characters psychologically understandable would be to humanize them, to undermine their stature as instruments of darkness, and therefore to erase the theme of opposition to the Implacable.

About Tyranny

For those who would turn their eyes away from the ultimate and prefer a smaller and more comfortable theme, Cormier has thoughtfully provided an alternative. It is possible to view the book as an examination of tyranny. The pattern overlaps, but is not identical. Seen this way, the trinity has a different cast. There are three structures of misused power: the school, as headed by Brother Leon; the athletic department, as headed by the coach; and the mob, as headed by Archie. Each has a passive assistant to tyranny, characters who have decent impulses but are ineffectual because they lack the courage to act. Obie is Archie's reluctant stooge; Carter agrees with the coach's approval of violence; and Brother Jacques despises Leon but condones his actions by not opposing. Shadowy outlines of the Government, the Military, and the Church might appear in this interpretation.

The question ultimately turns back, no matter whether tyranny or absolute evil is the enemy, to "How can we resist?" If evil had inherent power, there would be no answer. But Leon, Archie, and Emile all find their power source in their victim's own weaknesses. Leon even plays contemptuously with it in the classroom, when he tells the boys that they have become Nazi Germany by their fearful silence. Emile has very early discovered that most people want peace at any price and will accept almost any embarrassment or harassment rather than take a stand or make a fuss. "Nobody wanted trouble, nobody wanted to make trouble, nobody wanted a showdown." Archie, too, has realized that "the world was made up of two kinds of people—those who were victims and those who victimized." But the moment Jerry, of his own volition, refuses to sell the chocolates, he steps outside this cynical definition. In that is the source of hope.

Jerry at first has no idea why he has said no. "He'd wanted to end the ordeal—and then that terrible *No* had issued out of his mouth." But Jerry's life has been "like a yawning cavity in his chest" since his mother's death. His father is sleepwalking through his days, a man for whom everything and nothing is "Fine!"; a pharmacist who once wanted to be a doctor and now denies even that such an ambition ever existed. Like Prufrock, he is too numb to live and too afraid to act. When Jerry looks into the mirror he is appalled to see his father's face reflected in his own features. The hippie and the poster dare him to disturb the universe, and when he finally says no he is taking a stand against far more than a chocolate sale. And it is Brother Leon himself who has taught Jerry that not to resist is to assist.

Jerry is the *only one* who has learned that lesson, and this is what makes his destruction inevitable. Evil is implacable and merciless to a lone hero, in spite of the folk myth to the contrary. But could it have turned out differently? What if the marble had been black? Or Jerry's first blow had knocked Emile out? But these would have been arbitrary tamperings by the author. Ironically, the key to the real triumph of good comes again from Brother Leon. If others had joined Jerry. . . . There are a number of places in the story where this might have happened. The Goober, of course, is often on the verge of acting on his friendship for Jerry, but in the end, like Hamlet, he only thinks, and doesn't act until too late. For a moment he even hopes that it will all end in a stalemate. The Goober speaks for all the others in wanting to avoid confrontation at any cost. Obie might have acted on his disgust for Archie: "I owe you one for that!" he thinks when pushed too far. In the end he settles only for hoping that fate will punish Archie with a black marble. Carter, too, might have used his simple strength to end it.

Any of these isolated actions might have started the group movement that would have saved Jerry and defeated Leon and the Vigils. Even without such a spur the school comes close to following Jerry's example at the midpoint in the sale. But the motivation is negative—they are tired of selling—and selfishly individual—"let each one do his own thing." Without a conscious joining together for the good of all, they can easily be maneuvered separately back into doing the Vigils' will.

So here at last is Cormier's meaning. As one critic has written, "Jerry's defeat is unimportant. What is important is that he made the choice and that he stood firm for his convictions." Only by making that gesture can we hold on to our humanity, even when defeat is inevitable. But there is more—when the agents of evil are other human beings, perhaps good can win if enough people have the courage to take a stand together. Evil alliances are built with uneasy mutual distrust, but only goodness can join humans with the self-transcending strength of sympathy and love.

The Chocolate War Is About Changing Male Roles in the 1960s and 1970s

Yoshida Junko

Yoshida Junko is a literary critic specializing in children's literature.

In the following selection, Yoshida Junko examines The Chocolate War *from the perspective of the social and cultural changes occurring in the 1960s and 1970s. The rapid pace of social change in this era created a crisis in masculine identity, according to Junko, who contends that in* The Chocolate War, *by refusing to conform to peer pressure, Jerry is rebelling against gender stereotypes.*

The first paragraph of Robert Cormier's *The Chocolate War* (1974) is metaphorical: "They murdered him. As he turned to take the ball, a dam burst against the side of his head and a hand grenade shattered his stomach." We are immediately exposed to this violent scene without any knowledge of who "he" is, who "they" are, or what this scene is about. As the story unfolds, we learn that Jerry Renault, the protagonist, is involved in a conflict called the "chocolate war." But what is Jerry fighting against? And who or what is the enemy? On one hand, Patricia J. Campbell places the story in a moral context: "What he is opposing is not Brother Leon, not Archie, not Emile, but the monstrous force that moves them ... evil." Anne Scott MacLeod, on the other hand, maintains that Cormier's novels are "political novels" because he "is far more interested in the systems by which a society operates

Yoshida Junko, "The Quest for Masculinity in *The Chocolate War*: Changing Conceptions of Masculinity in the 1970s," *Children's Literature*, vol. 26, 1998, pp. 105–23. Copyright © The Johns Hopkins University Press 1998. Reproduced by permission.

than he is in individuals." I prefer to place *The Chocolate War* in a social and cultural context, reading it as a novel about changing conceptions of masculinity during the turbulent 1960s and early 1970s.

Jerry Seeks a Masculine Identity

Many sociologists view masculinity as a set of behaviors and attitudes that are constructed and maintained by a complex system of rewards and punishments. According to Arlene Skolnick, the sociocultural changes of the '60s were rooted in the unexpressed discontents of the '50s. In the mid-'70s, stimulated by the second wave of feminism, various men's movements began to develop.... "The various men's movements argued over conflicting ideals of masculinity. In fact, sociologist Kenneth Clatterbaugh identifies eight perspectives ranging from the 'conservative' to the evangelical Christian." Nonetheless, America's cultural anxiety about masculinity was based on a narrow image of the white middle-class heterosexual male. As in the film *Rebel Without a Cause* (1955), this image often caused a "masculinity crisis," for such men were expected to conceal their vulnerabilities, suppress their emotions, provide for their families, control their women, and, at the same time, be democratic and affectionate husbands and fathers. In other words, "the ideology of the strong male was at odds with the ideology of togetherness."

This masculinity crisis is deeply connected to unease about the feminine side of masculinity. As the sociologist E. Anthony Rotundo shows in his book *American Manhood*, the concept of masculinity is defined by the notion of a "separate sphere," which has become the norm for American society. This sphere excludes any attributes that are thought to be feminine, such as the nurturing, the caring, the intimate, and the emotional. As though to reflect the omission of the feminine from this conventional notion of masculinity, Cormier's *The Chocolate War* lacks major female characters except for Jerry's dead mother. The story unfolds in the all-male world of Trinity School. This unnatural absence of females in the novel emphasizes a masculinity that has excluded the feminine. Cormier is daring enough to portray the all-male world as bleak, to find fault with traditional gender roles, and to depict his protagonist, Jerry, as seeking a new male identity.

I would first like to examine the novel as a mythological quest story in which a young man seeks a masculine identity. Percival's quest in Arthurian legend is one of the most representative stories in which a fatherless young man leaves his mother and sets out to seek adventure. Because of his upbringing in the depths of the forest, Percival is ignorant of the outside world and, especially, of the power politics in the men's world. His encounter with the wounded Fisher King, whose kingdom is barren, is a crucial incident in his quest. When Percival witnesses a procession of Grail objects at a banquet, he misses a chance to ask specific questions, one of which is "Whom does the Grail serve?" Later Percival learns from his cousin of a legend predicting that an innocent fool would wander into the castle and ask questions by means of which he would heal the Fisher King. After wandering many years, Percival meets the Hideous Damsel, who reminds him of his failure to ask questions, thus prompting him to resume his Grail quest. Finally, he encounters an old hermit who reminds him a third time of his failure and its relation to his abandoned mother's death. Although Chrétien de Troyes's "Le Roman de Perceval, ou le conte du graal [The Novel of Percival, or the Tale of the Grail]," one of the oldest stories of Percival, ends at this point, many scholars presume that he returns to the Fisher King and questions him. As a result the wounded king is miraculously healed and the Waste Land becomes fertile again.

Among the many Jungian interpretations of this story as a boy's quest for masculinity, Robert A. Johnson's is especially insightful. From a feminist point of view, however, Johnson's focus on Percival's "homespun garment," a gift from his mother, is problematical. Johnson regards the garment as a metaphor for the mother complex in relation to Percival's failure to ask the questions. Instead, I see a connection between this failure of Percival's and the death of his abandoned mother, a connection made by two different characters: the cousin and the old hermit. From a feminist perspective, the healing of the wounded Fisher King is closely connected with Percival's reconciliation with his dead mother. In other words, reconciling with the feminine is essential for the rebirth of masculinity. . . .

Roots in Sixties Radicalism

The Chocolate War, in the same vein, unfolds as a boy's quest for a masculine identity. Jerry Renault, who lost his mother half a year before, is now being initiated into an all-male world, Trinity School, and is on his way to establishing his masculinity. Jerry's problem derives from the fact that his father is devastated by the loss of his wife and therefore cannot give adequate attention and care to his son. In other words, Jerry is a psychically fatherless son at a significant point in his development. Commenting on such situations, the psychoanalyst Guy Corneau maintains that the "lack of attention from the father results in the son's inability to identify with his father as a means of establishing his own masculine identity." Such fatherless sons "tend either to idealize the father or to seek an ideal father-substitute." To make matters worse, Jerry, who is portrayed as a "skinny kid," cannot find an ideal model of masculinity even in his all-male world. Janza and Carter, his macho peers, are too physically tough to be adequate role models, nor can Jerry conform to the conventional model of masculinity represented by Archie and Brother Leon.

While Jerry is suffering from the trauma caused by his mother's death, he is thrown into "the chocolate war" by vice principal Brother Leon, who compels the students to sell chocolates as part of their annual fund-raising effort. Archie Costello, the leader of the students' secret society, "The Vigils," gives Jerry an "assignment" to refuse to sell the chocolates. By giving assignments to his peers, Archie forces them to rebel against school authority, especially Brother Leon. Jerry's ultimate refusal to sell the chocolates drives him into isolation at school, especially in Brother Leon's class. Jerry knows that his rebellion is not against the chocolate sales but against the conformity underlying this activity. He says to himself, "It would be so easy, really, to yell 'Yes.' To say, 'Give me the chocolates to sell, Brother Leon.' So easy like the others, not to have to confront those terrible eyes every morning." . . .

Aaron Esman sheds light on the relationship between Brother Leon and the Vigils when he argues that adolescent rebellion during the tumultuous '60s did not derive from a "generation gap" but rather from efforts to live up to their elders' expectations. According to Esman, "the 'young radicals' . . . were, in most cases, expressing in an intensified form the liberal, antiauthoritarian view of their parents, who in many cases supported and encouraged their children's supposed 'rebellion.' . . . Most adolescents in most cultures conform rather quietly to the expectations of their elders." Jerry learns from three illuminating encounters or observations that his assigned role is not to rebel at all but to conform to his peer group. To begin with, a hippie who meets him only once at a bus stop criticizes him for his passive conformity, saying he is "middle-aged at fourteen, fifteen. Already caught in a routine." In fact, Jerry is afraid to become like his middle-aged father, who after his wife's death lives in a "gray drabness." Jerry cannot help but ask, "Was this all there was to life, after all?" and we are told that "now he [can] see his father's face reflected in his own features." Next the quotation on a poster, "Do I dare disturb the universe?" from T.S. Eliot's "The Love Song of J. Alfred Prufrock," urges Jerry to rebel against the whole school and "disturb the universe." Finally, when he sees his best friend

Goober exploited by Archie, Jerry recognizes that the assignment, despite its rebellious appearance, requires nothing but conformity to the Vigils.

Both Jerry's and Prufrock's questions are radical ones, posed by males who need to grow emotionally in order to escape their bleak situations. And, just as Percival is rebuked for his failure to ask the right questions, Jerry is challenged by the hippie and the poster to ask the right questions in the face of the suffering man and the Waste Land. When Jerry finally says no of his own will, however, his question takes the form of rebellion against the conventional masculinity embodied in both Brother Leon and Archie. On the eleventh day of his assignment, when he is supposed to say yes, Jerry declares, "'No. I'm not going to sell the chocolates.' Cities fell. Earth opened. Planets tilted. Stars plummeted. And the awful silence." At last Jerry has disturbed the universe. The only way Jerry has been able to establish his gender identity has been by arming himself with stubbornness and by fighting against conformity. Thus, even though Jerry has no positive role models at home or at school, he inaugurates his quest for masculinity by staging his own rebellion. So great is the difficulty of challenging the status quo in total isolation that Jerry's quest virtually becomes a war.

The Manipulation of Power

As *The Chocolate War* unfolds, it becomes clear that the type of conventional masculinity embodied in Leon and Archie is power-oriented. As their status as vice principal and vice president of their respective groups suggests, both of them are ambitious. Thus, despite their external differences, they are quite similar in their attempts to pursue power. Perry Nodelman points out that all the characters are "obsessively concerned with the chocolate sale" because that is "the showcase" where power is exercised and displayed. In Leon's daily roll call, for example, students are not allowed to respond to their names without accepting the chocolates and reporting their sales. In the students' eyes, Leon is a tyrant who stands on top of the hierarchy: "Everyone could see that Brother Leon was enjoying himself. This is what he liked—to be in command and everything going smoothly, the students responding to their names smartly, accepting the chocolates, showing school spirit." Archie is no different from Leon in his orientation to power. As Campbell points out, "arch" means "principal or chief": he is another tyrant in his realm, that of the Vigils, who, Cormier writes, "were the school. And he, Archie Costello, was The Vigils." And when Archie sells all the chocolates, he is "on top again . . . in charge once more, the entire school in the palm of his hand." It is to this power-hungry masculinity that Jerry says no, starting the war.

Such power as Archie and Brother Leon wield, which has particular features and patterns, warrants a closer look. First, their power is exercised through controlling information. Archie has Obie record personal information on all the students at the school. "His notebook was more complete than the school's files. It contained information, carefully coded, about everyone at Trinity." Archie thus manipulates information instead of threatening others by physical power and avoids using violence as much as possible. Archie explains, "I usually lay off the strong-arm stuff in the assignments. The brothers would close us down in no time and the kids would really start sabotaging if we started hurting people." He is afraid that violence might reveal his manipulation of power. And visibility might threaten the existence of the Vigils at Trinity.

Archie's manipulation of psychology and information demonstrates his awareness of a principle that [French philosopher] Michel Foucault identifies in *Discipline and Punish*: "The power exercised on the body is conceived not as a property, but as a strategy, that its effects of domination are attributed not to 'appropriation,' but to dispositions, maneuvers, tactics, techniques, functionings; . . . In short this power is exercised rather than possessed; it is not the 'privilege,' acquired or preserved, of the dominant class, but the overall effect of its strategic position." To put it another way, power is something manipulated in a political relationship; it cannot be obtained or possessed. Thus Foucault illustrates how "docile bodies" were constructed in the process of Western civilization by rulers' exercise of power within the institutionalized panopticism [all-seeing eye] of discipline and punishment, where a watchful eye is unceasingly vigilant for social deviates. The same was true of American society during the '50s, when there was a sort of McCarthyism with respect to gender roles. [Historian Robert L.] Griswold maintains that in the [post–World War II] era there was "conformity, a plague that infected middle-class men. . . . Men had become slaves to conformity." Conformity in the '50s, no doubt, worked as a shaper of conventional manhood. And there was no more perfect place to socialize white middle-class adolescent boys into conformity than prep schools such as Trinity.

Archie, as the leader of the Vigils, is aware of the principle of discipline and punishment in every detail of school life and manipulates people best by only hinting at the possibility of force. That is why he hates to see Janza and Carter exercise physical power, although he relies on them as a threat of violence. In this way, Archie meticulously distances himself from such a macho image. For example, he hates "the secretions of the human body, pee or perspiration" and "betraying an emotion" such as anger. The ideal image of masculinity for Archie is an isolated man "in harness," "cool" and "in command," with a poker face, who uses his brain instead of his body. Leon exercises power in a similar way, using his eyes and his pointer to manipulate his subjects, "watch[ing] the class like a hawk, suspicious, searching out cheaters or daydreamers, probing for weaknesses in the students and then exploiting those weaknesses." Leon is consistently portrayed as one who gazes from the top of the hierarchical power structure. Like Archie,

Leon avoids intimacy with the students, insisting that a "line must be drawn between teachers and students ... that line of separation must remain." Leon's exercise of power, represented by his hawklike, ever-vigilant eyes and his isolation from students, resembles the Vigils' panopticism.

Power-Hungry Men Are Dehumanized

The type of masculinity described above—one that manipulates power and, at the same time, is manipulated and constructed by power—has several problems. First, a man who adopts such a masculinity consciously or unconsciously suppresses his emotions and is therefore dehumanized and disindividualized. Just as Archie is portrayed as an impassive man who tries to erase the proof of his human body (urine or perspiration), Leon's existence is often reduced to his most prominent physical feature, his moist and hawklike eyes, thus obliterating his personality. He epitomizes what [author Marc Feigen] Fasteau calls "the male machine," whose "armor plating ... is virtually impregnable. His circuits are never scrambled or overrun by irrelevant personal signals. ... His relationship with other male machines is one of respect but not intimacy." Brother Leon has taken the conventions of masculinity so far that he seems at times an automaton [robot]. In *The Hazard of Being Male* the psychologist Herb Goldberg issues a warning to "men who live in harness." From the standpoint of the men's liberation movement, he stresses men's oppression more than women's: "They have lost touch with, or are running away from, their feelings and awareness of themselves as people. They have confused their social masks for their essence and they are destroying themselves while fulfilling the traditional definitions of masculine-appropriate behavior. ... Their reality is always approached through these veils of gender expectations." This passage seems an accurate description of Brother Leon.

A second problem with conventional masculinity is its tendencies toward isolation and dominance over others. As demonstrated by Archie and Leon, a man with this type of masculinity is isolated from others by his position at the top of the hierarchy. As the feminist psychologist Carol Gilligan points out in her *In a Different Voice,* males tend to form hierarchical relationships, separating themselves from other males in order to gain power, whereas females tend to form weblike interdependent networks. As a result, the masculinity constructed through the exercise of power began to acquire stereotypical images: it was seen as aggressive, emotionless, dehumanized, disindividualized, isolated, and incapable of intimacy. Consequently, by the time *The Chocolate War* was published, the various men's movement groups were trying to dispel this myth of masculinity. . . .

Condemning Conventional Masculinity

This social environment, however, was not necessarily a favorable one for adolescents attempting to establish a masculine identity. In the case of *The Chocolate War,* refusing to conform, that is, choosing to disturb the universe, means that Jerry himself is thrown into chaos. When he opens his locker to find it vandalized and is attacked by his peers, he finally understands the meaning of disturbing the universe: he has disturbed the norm for manhood in his society. The disturbed locker is a metaphor for both Jerry's inner disturbance and the disturbed norm of manhood at the school. This confusion is further reflected in Jerry's bewildered response to a violent attack by the school bullies, Janza and his buddies. Overwhelmed by the desire for revenge, Jerry identifies himself with the macho image of violent manhood. What is worse, he goes on to confront Janza physically in the boxing ring and temporarily becomes intoxicated with the thrill of physical violence. But then, a "new sickness invaded Jerry, the sickness of knowing what he had become, another animal, another

101

beast, another violent person in a violent world, inflicting damage, not disturbing the universe but damaging it." Cormier thus successfully demonstrates the violent and dark side of masculinity and provides readers with a powerful indictment of conventional manhood.

Jerry's violent response expresses his understanding of power and masculinity. He mistakenly believes that he can gain power and manliness if he physically confronts Janza, that power is some entity of which he can be robbed, and that gaining hierarchical power is masculine. Jerry eventually realizes that this masculine identity is self-defeating. Note that a similar motif can be found in the story of Percival when he encounters and kills the Red Knight. According to Johnson, "The Red Knight is the shadow side of masculinity, the negative, potentially destructive power. To truly become a man the shadow personality must be struggled with, but it cannot be repressed." This passage is also reminiscent of the vital scene in *A Wizard of Earthsea* in which Ged confronts the shadow. He names and accepts it as part of himself, just as Jerry later recognizes and calls himself "another beast, another violent person."

Jerry calls his recognition of his deep psychological wound "knowledge." It is the knowledge that he should not have disturbed the universe, that he should have conformed, that he should have continued to play aggressive masculine sports such as football. Thus the novel ends with Jerry's despairing warning to Goober, "Don't disturb the universe," which is also a spiritual death sentence pronounced on himself. In other words, Jerry is "murdered" by other males on the all-male "field," as is metaphorically depicted in the opening scene. In this sense, Jerry seems to be an "American Adam," R.W.B. Lewis's term for the innocent, isolated, nonconformist hero so common in American literature, especially the one in "the party of Irony," who suffers a "Fortunate Fall" on his way to maturation. *The Chocolate War* ends at the very nadir of the hero's fall, however; there is no happy ending, no rebirth of the hero. As MacLeod writes, "Cormier has abandoned an enduring American myth." Even in *The Catcher in the Rye*, which also ends unhappily, Holden Caulfield is not "murdered." Although psychologically weakened and wounded, Caufield escapes into a world of innocence, allowing [critic] Edgar Branch to say with some justification that Caulfield embodies the "myth of American youth." Similarly, Rebecca Lukens criticizes *The Chocolate War* in comparison with *The Catcher in the Rye*: "Holden finds that he is his own best hope for the phoniness of adult life. Cormier's characters come to no such faith. They are left without hope. The world grew darker between 1951 and 1974. Both writers skillfully create a realistic picture of the adolescent world, but unlike Salinger[,] who offers discovery, Cormier offers only despair."

From a feminist perspective on changing masculinity, however, I do not share this opinion. We cannot simply charge that Cormier offers us only despair or a hopeless world but instead must ask: Why does Caulfield survive as an American Adam, while Jerry is "murdered"? An answer lies in the fate of the "Earth Mother," described by Goldberg in *The Hazards of Being Male* as "fragile, helpless, and dependent, modest, pure, sexless, and unworldly." The Earth Mother—the externalized and institutionalized feminine nature—was alive and well in the 1950s because, during the postwar marriage rush and baby boom, "the gender-based division of labor at the heart of male breadwinning remained more or less unquestioned," even if some, like Caulfield, suspected the phoniness of such manhood. While Caulfield complains of his "damn lonesome" feeling, he often seeks warmth, compassion, and affection in female characters such as Phoebe and Jane Gallagher. As long as women assumed the institutionalized role of the Earth Mother, men could safely escape into the realm of childhood, a metaphor of innocence, and remain American Adams.

Jerry Rebels Against Gender Stereotypes

But by the time *The Chocolate War* was published, the social climate had changed drastically. The Earth Mother was already dead to many of those who had believed in her. As Goldberg declared, "Earth mother is dead and now macho can die as well. The man can come alive as a full person." Many women questioned the gender-based division of labor and rejected the role of Earth Mother. But since many men excluded feminine nature from their construction of masculinity, death of the Earth Mother was even more critical. This crisis for manhood is implied in *The Chocolate War* by the death of Jerry's mother and by the description of the power-hungry hierarchical men's world as "rotten," consisting, in Archie's words, "of two kinds of people—those who [are] victims and those who [victimize]," those who are "greedy and [those who are] cruel."

It should be noted that in 1973, a year before the publication of *The Chocolate War*, the Vietnam War ended, and rumors of Watergate spread. According to the historian Peter N. Carroll, America was suffering a "raw, painful, unhealing wound" or "a gaping crack in the American identity" inflicted by the "dishonesty of the Vietnam War" and the Watergate scandal. Symptomatic of this "gaping crack," films of the period reflect the ongoing dispute over a new male image. According to the Japanese scholar of American culture Kamei Shunsuke, "So-called 'New Cinemas' without any conventional heroes were in vogue. There were no heroes who would fight for the country, society, and its citizens, or for the righteousness and peace, but those who indulge in sex and violence, or those who roam around without any explicit purpose. What *were* there were anti-heroes." Kamei further points out that, around the same period, the American hero was resurrected in the character of Rocky, played by Sylvester Stallone. As the popularity of Stallone's sequels and Rambo films show, this new hero was accepted by American society in general. Thus in the 1970s and 1980s two competing types of hero coexisted, and therefore it is no wonder that Jerry's quest for masculine identity ends not with a hopeful prospect for his future or the healing of his wounds but with his metaphorical death.

Cormier has objected to having his books labeled "realistic" just because they do not end happily:

> But does an unhappy ending alone make a novel realistic? ... I am more concerned with reality than realism in the novels. ... I wanted to bring to life people like Jerry Renault ... who appears for only one poignant moment. ... But first came the emotions and then the characters. Once the characters are created and they become as real to you as the people you stand in line with at the movies that night, you must follow the inevitability of their actions.

Cormier's interest lies in depicting characters' emotions sympathetically rather than in constructing a realistic environment for his characters. In other words, Cormier depicts the confused emotions of men who are thrown into intense transitional crises. Such a crisis is Jerry's rebellion against gender stereotypes, and it cannot be overemphasized that Cormier, in creating Jerry, became a pioneer for nonconformists like him. Cormier, however, has Jerry pay a high price for his rebellion: his psychic wound.

As the story of Percival suggests, Jerry's psychic wound, recalling the wounded king, is a necessary part of his quest. But the ending of *The Chocolate War* offers no sign of Jerry's wound being healed. So it remains for *Beyond the Chocolate War* (1985) to deal with Jerry's healing or rebirth. Read as accounts of a single quest, the two books actually constitute one story. As the sequel's title indicates, the author depicts a new masculinity "beyond" the old one, a masculinity that transcends the chaos of conflicting models. ...

In a sense, the fact that Troyes's story of Percival was left incomplete is symbolic. Just as many scholars since the twelfth century have had to imagine an ending for Percival's quest, so today we have to wonder what the ending will be for male youth's quest in a world of changing masculinities. But the second wave of feminism has brought us to the point where the direction of these changes cannot be backward. Clearly, the health and welfare of masculinity is closely connected with the acceptance of femininity. Cormier's *The Chocolate War*, with its acute and sympathetic sensitivity, stands as witness to the need for this connection.

The Chocolate War Breaks the Taboos of the Genre

Anne Scott MacLeod

Anne Scott MacLeod is professor emerita at the University of Maryland, College Park. She is the author of numerous books on children's literature, including A Moral Tale: Children's Fiction and American Culture.

In this selection, Anne Scott MacLeod describes Robert Cormier's teen novels as important but not great works of literature. She finds his works unusual in the world of young-adult fiction, which is generally concerned with personal issues while Cormier's concerns are political. She points out that in The Chocolate War *and his other teen novels Cormier breaks most of the taboos of the young-adult genre, especially eschewing a victorious hero who wins out in the end.*

Robert Cormier is a conspicuous oddity in his chosen field. Writing for the adolescent reader, he has departed from standard models and broken some of the most fundamental taboos of that vocation. Each of his hard-edged novels for the young goes considerably beyond the standard limits of "contemporary realism" to describe a world of painful harshness, where choices are few and consequences desperate. Moreover, his novels are unequivocally downbeat; all three violate the unwritten rule that fiction for the young, however sternly realistic the narrative material, must offer some portion of hope, must end at least with some affirmative message. Affirmation is hard to find in Cormier's work, and conventional hopefulness is quite irrelevant to it.

But while these sharp breaks with accepted practice have been much noted by reviewers, and have furnished Cormier's

Anne Scott MacLeod, "Robert Cormier and the Adolescent Novel," *Children's Literature in Education*, vol. 12, no. 2, Summer 1981, pp. 74–81. Copyright © 1981. Reproduced with kind permission from Springer Science and Business Media and the author.

reputation for bleakness, curiously little notice has been taken of another, and, to my mind, equally interesting departure from the norm in his novels. Quite aside from his attitudes and conclusions, Cormier is a maverick in the field of adolescent literature because he is writing what are, at bottom, political novels. George Orwell once claimed that there is no such thing as a "genuinely nonpolitical literature," but the dictum seems to me inapplicable to most writing for young adults. A consistent feature of almost the whole body of adolescent literature is its isolation from the political and societal, its nearly total preoccupation with personality. The typical adolescent novel is wrapped tightly around the individual and the personal; questions of psychological development and personal morality dominate the genre. In fact, most authors of adolescent literature seem to take for their model adolescents themselves, with their paramount interest in self, individual morality, interior change, and personality.

Cormier, on the other hand, is far more interested in the systems by which a society operates than he is in individuals. His novels center on the interplay between individuals and their context, between the needs and demands of the system and the needs and rights of individuals—in other words, on the political context in which his characters, like all of us, must live. He is, obviously, concerned with moral questions, but the morality involved is of a wholly different order from the purely personal moral concerns of most teen novels.

Cormier's political cast of mind explains the relative unimportance of characterization in his work. Inner character is less to him than situation. In *Chocolate War*, for example, the wellsprings of Archie's evil are never adequately explained, and Jerry's motivation for his lonely rebellion, while plausible enough, is not dwelt upon at any great length. Certainly it is not the centerpiece of the narrative, as it would be in most teen novels. . . .

Adolf Hitler acknowledges frantic cheers from the German crowds. As in Nazi Germany, evil at Trinity School was empowered because the majority went along with it. Popperfoto/ Getty Images.

The book that has drawn the most critical attention [of all of Cormier's young-adult novels] is *Chocolate War*, possibly because it was the first, perhaps because its statement of defeat is explicit and made by the protagonist, or maybe simply because it is hard to recognize until the end just how shatteringly this novel differs from others of its genre. It looks, after all, like a school story, about school boys, and can be read just that way—in which case the unhappy comment by several reviewers about its negativism is understandable. But of course *Chocolate War* has another life outside its familiar form: it is a metaphor, a parable of political evil and a small manual on the sources and uses of political power.

The evil in *Chocolate War* is initiated by individuals, but not contained in them. Archie and Brother Leon are manipulators: Archie manipulates the Vigils, Brother Leon manipulates his students; together, during the chocolate sale, they manipulate the whole school. Yet neither could work his will without the cooperation of others. The acquiescence of the community is essential to their power, as the classroom scene makes clear. In an episode that is a virtual cliché in school stories, Brother Leon singles out a student for torment, accusing him of cheating, mocking and humiliating him, while the rest of the class laughs uncomfortably. If this were all, the scene would simply establish (without much originality) that Brother Leon is the kind of teacher who abuses the power of his position for some private satisfaction. But Cormier's interest here is not really Brother Leon, still less the reasons for his abuse of position. What he wants to demonstrate is the source of the power, which is, of course, the students themselves. The harassment goes on exactly as long as the class lets it; when at last one student speaks up in mild protest, the spell breaks. And it is Brother Leon himself who points out the moral, asking contemptuously why no one had objected sooner, suggesting the parallel with Nazi Germany.

Still, the message of the novel as a whole is neither so simple nor so hopeful as the episode might imply. If it were, then Jerry's lone dissent would succeed, would break the c ombined power of Archie and Brother Leon—and would place the novel squarely in the long American tradition of the triumphant lonely hero tale. Instead, there is that final scene which laid the cornerstone of Cormier's reputation for bleakness: Jerry carried away on a stretcher, his face too battered to allow him to speak the message he wants to convey to Goober. . . .

The lone dissent has not only failed, it is repudiated. The American Adam is brought low; Huck Finn turns Jim over to the slave-catchers, Gary Cooper [who plays the hero in the western *High Noon*] lies in his own blood in the street at high noon—no wonder the reviewers gasped. In one brief, bitter paragraph, Cormier has abandoned an enduring American myth to confront his teenaged readers with life as it more often is—with the dangers of dissent, the ferocity of systems as they protect themselves, the power of the pressure to conform....

Cormier's teen novels are not "great books"; I doubt that they will outlast their topical relevance. But they are important books just the same. Cormier writes of things few books for the young acknowledge at all. He has evoked a political world in which evil is neither an individual phenomenon nor a personality fault explainable by individual psychology, but a collaborative act between individuals and political systems which begins when the individual gives over to the system the moral responsibility that is part of being human. He suggests that innocence can be a moral defect, that evil is (as [German political theorist] Hannah Arendt has said) banal, and, above all, that political bureaucracies are often—perhaps always—a potential danger to individual freedom because they are fundamentally committed to their own perpetuation, which is always threatened by individual dissent....

Neither the issues Cormier poses nor the answers he implies belong to the same moral world as the themes of adjustment, acceptance, and understanding that undergird most adolescent fiction. Instead, his work opens again the complex questions of the function of literature and of whether that function varies with the age of the intended reader. Cormier's three adolescent novels answer for him....

The Desire to Be Accepted Compels People to Conform

David Rees

David Rees is a British author, lecturer, and reviewer who won the Carnegie Medal in 1978 for his book The Exeter Blitz.

In the following selection, David Rees argues that on the surface The Chocolate War *is a political book about power and corruption. However, at another level, it is about the conflict between individualism and peer pressure. According to Rees, Robert Cormier's message is that the desire to be accepted is a powerful force, especially in the teen years, and that it can be manipulated by those in power to cause harm.*

In recent years novels for the young adult have proliferated so much that one could almost call this particular market a growth industry, even though authors seem to have gone out of their way to stress the problems adolescents may be confronted by rather than the excitements and pleasures of this period of life. Unwanted pregnancies, drugs, abortion, crime and unsatisfactory parents all occur more frequently in teenage fiction than happy home backgrounds, fulfilling love affairs, or indeed the average preoccupations of most young people. One may easily sympathize with readers who vainly search for something that reflects life as they know it.

The Chocolate War Is About Compromise

One lesson that must be learned in the teenage years is that it is often necessary to compromise in order to survive; that the gap between the actual and the ideal has to be bridged; that,

David Rees, "The Sadness of Compromise: Robert Cormier and Jill Chaney," *Marble in the Water: Essays on Contemporary Writers of Fiction for Children and Young Adults*, Boston, MA: The Horn Book, 1980, pp. 155–72. Copyright © 1980 by The Horn Book, Inc., Boston, MA, www.hbook.com. All rights reserved. Reproduced by permission.

as Ben Blewitt comes to realize in Philippa Pearce's *A Dog So Small*, "if you didn't have the possible things, then you had nothing." Too often the hero in the teenage novel blames a malevolent hostile world for shortcomings that are his own, and emerges at the end of the story still convinced that he should turn his back on things rather than examine his own failings. Valuable, then, is the work of writers such as Robert Cormier and Jill Chaney, admittedly quite unlike in style, preoccupation, and achievement, but who are both concerned with the essential sadness of the inevitable passing from innocence to experience—the compromise of survival: Teenagers need to be able to say, "yes: so that's how you cope with it" and novels that *show them how* are likely to be more helpful to the imaginative and emotional growth of the young people than those that take issues—drugs, venereal disease, or whatever—as starting points.

The Chocolate War, Robert Cormier's first novel for young adults, is, on the surface, a political book. It is about power, power structures, corruption—about how absolute power corrupts absolutely. But, more subtly, beneath the surface, it is about compromise and the choice between hunting with the pack or searching for strength as an individual: about the toughness needed in the struggle to be a successful outsider. Jerry Renault, the central character, is a fascinating and complex creation, considerably more ambiguous than he initially appears to be. One may like him up to a point, and admire his heroic, if futile, refusal to join in the attempts that Brother Leon has organized to raise funds for his school by the sale of the chocolates. There is a strong temptation on the reader's part to identify with him, to agree with his version of events: but it's a temptation that should be resisted. There is much that it not admirable about Jerry Renault. His weakness is an overriding passion to conform to a conventional teenage image of machismo, which is seen mostly in his desire to become an admired member of the football team—looked up to, respected, a boy with a niche in society. He doesn't have any realization that such values are false; that conventional respect from others is no measure of real worth. A similar falseness exists in his attitude to the opposite sex; he wants a relationship with a girl not because it may be more interesting and satisfying than a friendship with another boy, but because

> The one devastating sorrow he carried within him was the fear that he would die before holding a girl's breast in his hand.

He is not the stuff of which heroes are made, and his final compromise is not the gesture of despair that some critics have suggested, but entirely characteristic:

> He had to tell Goober to play ball, to play football, to run, to make the team, to sell the chocolates, to sell whatever they wanted you to sell, to do whatever they wanted you to do . . . Don't disturb the universe, Goober, no matter what the posters say.

His stand against selling the chocolates is an aberration, quite uncharacteristic of him, and it is interesting that Cormier does not give the reader an adequate explanation for Jerry's decision to opt out in this matter. Goober is much more naturally an outsider type than Jerry, and though his appearance in the book is disappointingly fleeting, Cormier would have manufactured a much less worthwhile novel if he had made Goober the central character, for it would have become a rather conventional struggle between good and evil.

A Subtle Message

The Chocolate War is not an entirely satisfactory book. Goober is not the only person left undeveloped; the author shows us the thinking processes of too many of his characters, and he flits more rapidly than he should from one to another; the writing is at times too purple, especially in the scenes of physical violence. One wonders if the author may be enjoying these scenes a little, and, I feel, he may also share Jerry's belief in a false idea of masculine values. The evil characters, Archie and Brother Leon, are so one-dimensionally villainous that they are no more than caricatures. They present a considerable threat to the reader's ability to believe in the reality of what he is being told. But the central theme—to conform or not to conform—is handled with great skill, and the book's message is more subtle than it seems: Cormier is not saying that the might of evil institutions inevitably corrupts good people, but that the desire to be accepted is a major weakness which can easily be exploited by the wicked.

The Chocolate War Is About the Misuse of Power

Theodore Weesner

Theodore Weesner is a book reviewer and author of the novel The Car Thief.

Although he admits that The Chocolate War *can be faulted for its two-dimensional characters, Theodore Weesner maintains in the following essay that it delivers a powerful message about the use of power. This novel is Robert Cormier's first book aimed at a young-adult audience, and Weesner asserts that the author has written it in a way to engage provocative classroom discussions on the appropriate exercise of power in a society.*

Robert Cormier's fourth novel, written for teen-agers but a strong read for adults, is a story with a highly serious message not only about the usurpation and misuse of power but about power's inevitable staying. *The Chocolate War* is masterfully structured and rich in theme; the action is well crafted, well timed, suspenseful; complex ideas develop and unfold with clarity. The novel may be faulted only for its general short-changing of character. The characters are quick studies, recognizable at a glance, two dimensional.

An Alliance of Power

No less than 20,000 boxes of cheap chocolates create war conditions in the mini-society of a private Catholic day school for boys. An ambitious, evil, intensely effective teacher who aims to be headmaster of this universe, Brother Leon, has picked up the chocolates for a shady song and is determined to make a killing and take his giant stride to power. His vehicle is the school's annual fundraising campaign, his captive salesmen are the students—50 boxes apiece at $2 a box—and his methods range from sales-incentive hype to direct and indirect intimidation, the administering of power.

Of course the task is nearly impossible, and with an aficionado's appreciation for control and cruelty the good Brother courts as ally the school's secret society, The Vigils, a group dedicated to inflicting humiliations and tortures, "assignments" on others. The Vigils, whose mere existence, prior to Brother Leon, has never been admitted by school officials, is, not surprisingly, made up of the bullies, the animals and hangers-on of adolescence. But the group becomes special here for it has at its head the legendary Archie Costello, who may be one of the most brilliantly malicious high school seniors ever imagined.

On the other side, weighing in for the good guys—clearly underweight and mildly underprivileged—is Jerry Renault, a perplexed freshman and an obvious victim. He weighs in by accident, however, for his initial act of defiance—he says no to selling his 50-box quota—is merely one of Archie's assignments, which are intended to show Brother Leon and the every-straying Vigils where the power actually resides. At the daily roll-call, when each student must call out his sales for the previous day, Jerry Renault alone says "No."

Word gets around that the act is nothing more than an exercise of Archie's cool, a little shoving at the shoulder of Brother Leon; but Jerry, pushed around too much already, troubled by the fact of his father being pushed around always in the real world and seeing this may well be of the real world, gets a taste for the pleasure of defiance—it is sweet and restorative—and sets off, alone, in a way reminiscent of the profound loneliness of Alan Sillitoe's defiant long-distance runner. Day after day, he says "No."

A group of Iraqi children training for war pose before a portrait of Iraq's dictator Saddam Hussein in 1990. Tyrants often use their power to exploit the vulnerability of youth. AP Images.

Begrudged admiration nurtures respect, and respect begins to arouse an outright following. Signs appear: *Screw the Chocolates and Screw the Vigils.* Sales drop. And drop. Brother Leon and Archie, confronted by a quality in human nature they have themselves caused to emerge have a rebellion on their hands. They may not altogether comprehend or appreciate the quality of mind in rebellion, but of course they know about the application of power, and thus, only slightly panicked do they bring their larger weapons to bear.

No Easy Answer

The stuff of this novel is serious, however, and although a mushy, carameled battle is expected, and although humorous scenes do precede the novel's denouement, an easy out does not occur. Rather, like most rebellions, the action here is turned rather quickly, and there with a disturbing impact is the point, the message of the story and the conclusion of the novel.

The Chocolate War, presenting as it does a philosophical plateau between childhood and adulthood, seems an ideal study for the high school classroom. The characters, although not deeply drawn, are accurate and touch close enough to raise questions of identification, questions of one's location within an arena of power, and also provide some hard recognition of the functions of power within a society. A scene, frightening in its overtones, shows Brother Leon persuading a classroom that its star pupil is in fact a cheat and a liar. Of course the boy is neither—the character assassination is merely one of Brother Leon's odd teaching devices—but the class is swayed and a message in extension of the larger theme is delivered. When the story ends, one wishes only that one had known the characters better, to better understand their responses to the importance of the message.

The Chocolate War
Is Not Realistic

Norma Bagnall

Norma Bagnall is a member of the Department of English at Texas A&M University.

Norma Bagnall considers The Chocolate War *an example of a depressing trend in recent children's literature to write about only the ugly side of life and term it "realistic." She doesn't find the book realistic because Jerry is the only good kid, there are no adults worth emulating, and the language and imagery are ugly. It is a disturbing book for teens, she attests, because it presents a vision of hopelessness that is distorted and unhealthy.*

Recently we have seen a trend in literature for young people that some call realism, but in fact it is not realistic at all. Realism is an honest attempt to picture people and events as they really are. To portray things from the brutal or dark side only, as is being done in current literature, is no more realistic than presenting only those sweet and idealistic stories of an earlier age.

Only the Ugly Side of Life

As an example, *The Chocolate War*, by Robert Cormier, is described as a realistic junior novel, and it meets some of the requirements for realism. Cormier has written honestly, I believe, what he thinks could happen at a private boys' school in the 1970s when one student decides to flout the system. Such honesty is basic to realism. He has also structured the novel masterfully; each incident builds up independently of the oth-

Norma Bagnall, "Realism: How Realistic Is It? A Look at *The Chocolate War*," *Top of the News*, vol. 36, no. 2, Winter 1980, pp. 214–17. Copyright © 1980 by the American Library Association. Reproduced by permission.

ers, yet each contributes strength to the structure of the story, all with careful understatement. Cormier knows his craft; he has written a compelling novel.

But it is not realistic. In it there are no adults worth emulating; Jerry is the only decent kid, and he is victimized by his peers, with the cooperation of school officials. Only the ugly is presented through the novel's language, actions, and imagery; goodness and honor are never rewarded. Love and concern for other people is ignored, and hopelessness pervades the entire story. The presentation of people and events shows only the evil, the ugly, and the sordid. It is not appropriate for young people because it presents a distorted view of reality and because it lacks hope.

Of the adults in *The Chocolate War* Brother Leon is the very portrayal of evil, the malevolent force who controls the school, since the headmaster is conveniently out of the way, ill and in the hospital (almost the cliché of the dead mother in young people's stories, including this one). The other teachers? Brother Eugene, done in by the destruction of his classroom, falls apart just as surely as the classroom furniture did. Brother Jacques at first seems honorable, but because he is weak, he remains subservient to Brother Leon.

The other adults? Jerry's father, torn by grief over the death of his wife, is separated from Jerry except for whatever contact is necessary in their living together. Their separation had been a physical one the previous summer when Jerry lived with cousins following his mother's death; we know we can expect little more from Mr. Renault. The other parents in the book are stereotypes, praising their children for trivial accomplishments, ignoring them most of the time. All are vapid and depressing.

And the kids. Archie is Brother Leon's counterpart among the boys; it is his cunning that makes him a leader. Jerry is the only honorable boy, the only boy with the guts to be a nonconformist, to stand up to the bullies who rule the school. We think at first that Goober will be honorable and an ally in this brutal war, but he is not; rather he is one of those people who want to "shrivel into invisibility" rather than make trouble, or face trouble.

The other kids run the gamut from those who do anything to conform to rules set up by the bullies, to the bullies themselves, who intimidate, humiliate, and harass the weaker boys. All are shaped by the society at Trinity High; all are trapped by a cruel, ugly, sadistic system.

Ugly Language and Actions

The language in the novel is ugly as well. It has become popular to "tell it like it is," and for some writers this means including the crude slang we know kids use. So Cormier uses much of it, but generally it is appropriate to its context and will probably not disturb the book's readers; kids can handle four-letter-words with greater ease than my generation can. However, I don't think it is necessary for a writer for young adults to feed back to them their own slang any more than it is necessary for a writer for five-year-olds to include the bathroom language he or she knows five-year-olds use and find titillating.

The actions of the characters are almost without exception ugly, exemplifying only the most sordid side of their natures. Our senses are assaulted by kids cringing, sniveling, humiliating each other, stealing, and bullying. There are frequent references to masturbation and vomiting. Jerry, in particular, vomits a lot, an ugly picture but one that is perhaps in keeping with the one-sided view the book presents. The adults' actions are not as sordid, but they are as depressing. They nag, drink, sleep, watch television; they are trapped in dull jobs; they do dull things. None are involved in anything worthwhile with their children. People, we are told by Archie, "are two things: greedy and cruel." Cormier's people certainly are.

Most of the imagery is deliberately ugly. The word "beautiful" is used repeatedly by Archie, but only in sarcasm. "Beautiful" describes his intimidation of another student or the chaos he [has] created. We are assailed with images of the unpleasant odors of vomit, sweat, pee, and Leon's breath. Leon's smile is "like the kind an undertaker fixes on the face of a corpse." Sweat, for Jerry, moves "like small moist bugs on his forehead." Nature imagery is especially unpleasant as the sunset becomes the "sun bleeding low in the sky and spurting its veins," and the autumn leaves fluttering to the ground are "like doomed and crippled birds."

A Distorted View of Humanity

The Chocolate War has been compared to *A Separate Peace* and to *Lord of the Flies*, which is expected. All deal with boys forming their own societal group complete with rules, taboos, value systems, and leaders—like any society.

But in *A Separate Peace* there are some sympathetic adults, adults to trust and to emulate. There is genuine, healthy rapport among the boys on the playing field. The book does not include tasteless language, and ugly incidents are limited to those essential to the story line. Finally, there are forgiveness and love to offset an otherwise harsh story.

Lord of the Flies tells an ugly story with cynical harshness, and it includes many ugly incidents and much ugly imagery, but it is set in a real jungle, on an island, with the boys completely cut off from adult intervention. *The Chocolate War* takes place in a large New England city, and involves more than eight hundred adults directly concerned with the society of boys. It goes beyond *Lord of the Flies* in that it suggests that adults are no more willing or capable of controlling their environment than are youngsters. It insinuates that it is possible that this many parents and teachers would be totally unconcerned about their own children or their students. It states not only that civilization can break down on an isolated island among a group of British school boys, but that it has broken down also for a large and diverse group of adults in a major American city.

This distorted view of humanity, this strange sense of what makes civilization work is hammered home by the conclusion of the story. Hints are given throughout that justice will finally triumph. Through foreshadowing we are led to believe that Jerry is going to win his battle, but this is just a trick of the author's.

We learn early in the story that Archie, as the "Assigner" of the Vigils—the leading group of boys at Trinity High—is kept in line by a box of marbles. He has pushed his luck for three years; he has never once drawn the black marble that would force him to carry out the assignments he gives to others. It is suggested in the story that "the law of averages may catch up to him; his luck may be running out." Another hint comes in the classroom when Brother Leon baits a weak student unmercifully until a voice from the back of the room interrupts with "Aw, let the kid alone," and we are led to believe that others, particularly if they can remain anonymous, will speak out for justice.

Later when Obie learns that Archie has taken Brother Jacques into his confidence, tricking the boys so that their reaction to the word *environment* was used against them instead of to bait the teacher, Obie is furious at Archie. He walks off thinking, "I owe you for that." We expect Obie to take some kind of action that will prevent Archie from remaining the school leader.

Still another hint of the eventual triumph of goodness comes after Jerry appears before the Vigils for the second time and Archie "asks" him to sell the chocolates. Obie can scarcely believe the word *asks*: "as if Archie was trying to bargain with the kid, *asking*, for crying out loud. I've got you, Archie, you bastard," Obie thinks. He "had never known such sweet victory. The goddam freshman was going to screw Archie up, at last." This is the final clue we need to believe that Jerry eventually will win.

But he does not win. He is brutally beaten and carried away broken and unconscious. The reader feels tricked. This completes Cormier's destruction of all that is good and honorable and becomes the most disturbing element in the book. Jerry, like us, is let down with a sickening thud.

So I struggle with *The Chocolate War*. I do not believe writers should be dictated to by librarians, by parents, by me, about what they should write. Yet I am disturbed by this book because, in spite of being brilliantly structured and skillfully written, it presents a distorted view of reality and a feeling of absolute hopelessness that is unhealthy. We know from the work of [humanistic psychologist] Abraham Maslow that people need a firmly based, high evaluation of themselves for their own self-respect and for the respect of others. We know they need positive experiences as well to mature wisely and well. There are no positive experiences in this book. We know also from the work of [psychologists] Curt Richter and Martin Seligman that we can teach hopelessness to our young if they are taught that no matter how hard they struggle they cannot win. This story teaches that hopelessness.

It is as inaccurate to present only the sordid and call it realistic as it has been in the past to present only the idealistic. It is probably even more damaging. *The Chocolate War* endorses and supports the thesis that one is better off not struggling for what is right because one cannot win and thus is, in effect, an object lesson in futility.

The Chocolate War Is Realistic

Betty Carter and Karen Harris

Betty Carter is a librarian at Spring Branch Independent School District in Houston, Texas, and Karen Harris is associate professor of library science at the University of New Orleans in Louisiana.

In the following selection, Betty Carter and Karen Harris find Norma Bagnall's characterization of The Chocolate War *as unrealistic and hopeless to be inaccurate and unwarranted. Bagnall focuses her attention solely on the plot, say Carter and Harris, who point out that Cormier is using his story as a vehicle to explore the nature of tyranny and evil. The literary and biblical allusions sprinkled throughout the text are evidence of his intentions that the book is not just about selling chocolates. Because he is focusing on tyranny and evil as his subjects, it makes sense that his message is a somber one, Carter and Harris assert. His ultimate message, however, is not without hope they contend.*

Norma Bagnall describes *The Chocolate War* as a hopeless novel about the forced sale of candy in a boys' parochial high school. She considers it an unrealistic picture of adolescent life and unsuitable reading material for teenagers. We think her description is inaccurate and her criticism unwarranted.

About the Nature of Tyranny

Cormier's novel is only superficially about the fund-raising activities at a Catholic institution; its greater concerns are with the nature and functioning of tyranny. While it demonstrates the inability of a decent individual to survive unaided in a

Betty Carter and Karen Harris, "Realism in Adolescent Fiction: In Defense of *The Chocolate War*," *Top of the News*, vol. 36, no. 3, Spring 1980, pp. 383–85. Copyright © 1980 by the American Library Association. Reproduced by permission.

corrupt and oppressive society, it does not imply that such defeat is inevitable. To see the book as something "which could happen at a private boys' school in the 1970s when one student decides to flout the system" is to confuse setting with substance and plot device with purpose.

Cormier persistently uses figurative language as one device to remind the reader that the meaning of the book is not limited to the confines of the story line or the campus of Trinity High. After Archie decides that Jerry Renault's first assignment will be to refuse to sell chocolates, Obie notices that "the shadows of the goal posts definitely resembled a network of crosses, empty crucifixes." This reference to the central symbol of Christianity should certainly suggest that more is at issue than merely the selling of chocolates. When Jerry, defying the Vigils, announces he still will not accept the candy, the effect is cataclysmic: "Cities fell. Earth opened. Planets tilted. Stars plummeted." The author has clearly moved the action from the campus to the cosmos.

The metaphorical quality of the three power structures within the school is spelled out specifically and hinted at obliquely. The most obvious symbol is the athletic department, which provides for the testing of individuals, including each one's willingness and ability to withstand physical abuse. The football field is an arena where violence is ritualized, sanctioned, and even demanded. After the brutal fight in which Jerry is physically beaten and psychologically destroyed, he warns his friend to "play ball." This metaphor, taken from sports, is not restricted to the game but encapsulates the lesson Jerry has so painfully learned: he had better cooperate with the power structure or he will be crushed.

Biblical and Literary Allusions

The school itself is a microcosm of society. In one of the most telling and ironic scenes in the story, the metaphorical implications of life at Trinity are baldly stated. Brother Leon accuses an "A" student, George Bailey, of cheating, humiliating him in front of his embarrassed but unprotesting classmates. Suddenly turning from his victim, he castigates the other students for not coming to the boy's defense. He likens them to the citizens of Germany who allowed the rise of Nazism, not through their support of Hitler, but through their inertia. His comparison is tragically prophetic.

Cormier further draws the reader outside the perimeters of a particular school by his frequent use of literary and biblical allusions. References to Hamlet [the title character of Shakespeare's play], Shylock [from Shakespeare's *The Merchant of Venice*], J. Alfred Prufrock [from T.S. Eliot's poem "The Love Song of J. Alfred Prufrock"], Saint Peter, Moses, and John the Baptist invite comparisons and underscore the persisting and timeless relevance of events.

The most significant object in the story is the poster in Jerry's locker that asks: Do I Dare Disturb the Universe? When Cormier introduces it he describes it in detail, suggesting through Jerry's uncertainty that the caption may be subject to various interpretations. The question does not remain idle, tucked away in Jerry's locker, but is raised repeatedly when anyone—Jerry, his father, his classmates, his teachers—either challenges or bows to the demands of the establishment. Jerry ponders, expands, and twists the quote, and as his definition of the universe grows and changes, he realizes he is not just a single individual but a part of an interlocking social order. Following Jerry's ruminations, readers gain similar insight into the book's intent and theme. Cormier is clearly not writing about this existential question solely within the context of an isolated secondary school, but as it is applicable to the larger world.

A Valid Picture of Human Behavior

Bagnall's criticism that *The Chocolate War* is not realistic is equally insupportable. She claims Cormier's work is distorted because "only the ugly is presented . . . goodness and honor are never rewarded."

[Critic] Northrop Frye claims that "the world of literature is a world where there is no reality except that 'of the human imagination. . . . There are two halves to literary experience. Imagination gives us both a better and a worse world than the one we usually live with, and demands that we keep looking steadily at them both." If Cormier chooses to concentrate on the "worse world," he is exercising a literary privilege claimed by many major writers since [ancient Greek playwright] Sophocles. Although this is not the only side of reality, it is certainly a significant one and remains a persisting concern of authors because it is a persisting component of human behavior.

It may be desirable for a library collection to encompass the full spectrum of human imagination, but such a comprehensive range cannot be reasonably required of every individual work. Condemning Cormier for ignoring the sunnier aspects of human behavior is as inappropriate as castigating [author Helen] Cresswell for avoiding serious matters in *The Bagthorpe Saga.*

Literary realism is not journalistic reporting. As Frye explains, "The poet's function is not to tell you what happened, but what happens: not what did take place, but the kind of thing that always does take place." Novelists, of course, are under the same constraints. They choose particular elements of the world—distill, concentrate, and juxtapose them in such a manner as to illuminate a particular facet of the human condition. This, it seems to us, is exactly what Robert Cormier accomplishes in his junior novels, remaining well within the tradition of literary realism.

In *The Chocolate War* he has chosen to focus on tyranny and evil—not as vague abstractions, but given flesh and substance in the persons of Brother Leon and Archie. Bagnall disapproves of Cormier's concentration on that which is displeasing and concludes that the book is inappropriate for youngsters because its language, actions, and imagery are ugly.

The unpleasant should not be confused with the unsuitable. Cormier's responsibility to his craft requires him to present characters and images, not as one would like them to be, but as they must be in order to make the novel and its message credible. Consequently, the language and images are disturbing, but then, so is tyranny. To mask evil with delicate similes would only diminish its potency, and to introduce a noble adult to save the day would truly be unrealistic.

Bagnall contends "*The Chocolate War* endorses and supports the thesis that one is better off not struggling for what is right because one cannot win and thus is, in effect, an object lesson in futility." Such a reading makes sense only if Jerry's destruction is inevitable. The reason Jerry was not saved was because he stood alone. But he need not have been alone, as Cormier states clearly and with consummate irony through the words of Brother Leon when he falsely accuses Bailey of cheating. The boys at Trinity could have come to Jerry's defense, if they had not lacked courage. Mr. Renault could have saved his son if he had not been so self-absorbed. The brothers could have checked Leon's ambitions if they had had the will. No one did. Jerry paid a terrible price for everyone else's inadequacies.

Robert Cormier does not leave his readers without hope, but he does deliver a warning: they may not plead innocence, ignorance, or prior commitments when the threat of tyranny confronts them. He does not imply that resistance is easy, but he insists it is mandatory.

The Chocolate War Is Too Brutal and Raw

Fred Inglis

Fred Inglis is emeritus professor of cultural studies at the University of Sheffield in England. He has published many books in the fields of literature, education, and cultural studies.

In the following selection, Fred Inglis suggests that the seeds of Robert Cormier's pessimistic view of life and his distrust of authority may have their roots in his radical 1960s past. For Inglis The Chocolate War *is a deeply disturbing book and inappropriate for children because of its hopeless message—that institutions hold power and people are powerless.*

The action [in *The Chocolate War*] is set in a private school of Catholic foundation in the States, and it is its American flavour which first strikes an English reader. This is partly its literary convention and diction—a grating, staccato mixture of [J.D.] Salinger's *The Catcher in the Rye* and its much less accomplished, more deliberately gruesome and unreflective successors in the graduate schools of creative writing for teenagers. But also, and more pervasively, its American quality comes out in the conventional determination to tear away all the conventions of writing for children. The hero is not victorious, he is broken and humiliated; the repressive Mafiosi who run the school have clenched their fists even more tightly upon their power; the story is remorselessly tense, and only loosens the tension momentarily in order to tighten it more frighteningly in a new corner—a sort of *Marathon Man* [a thriller novel by William Goldman] for children. The hero is

Fred Inglis, "Love and Death in Children's Novels," *The Promise of Happiness: Value and Meaning in Children's Fiction*, New York, NY: Cambridge University Press, 1981, pp. 271–91. Copyright © Cambridge University Press 1981. Reprinted with the permission of Cambridge University Press.

entirely a victim, but the more entirely a latter-day victim in that his victimization stands for nothing redemptive or suc-couring [saving] to others in his community. He is entirely solitary, and his defeat is only debilitating.

Authority Breaks the Individual's Spirit

But to judge in this way is to invite misunderstandings. My criticism is not simply a consequence of disliking and fearing the author's world-picture; it is obviously possible that the heroic resistance of individuals to evil and cruelty may be futile, and the fiction of the twentieth century furnishes many convincing examples: [Joseph] Conrad's *Nostromo* and Gabriel Marquez's *One Hundred Years of Solitude* are only two of the classics in the literature of oppression. What is deeply wrong with *The Chocolate War*, which is why I am considering it here, is its grossness and indelicacy in telling its child-readers that heroism is, strictly, such a dead end. Trapped by prose and convention within the hero's skull, the author can find no way to qualify the helpless narrowness of his vision, and give the reader some detachment from and purchase [advantage] on the hero's plight. This wouldn't matter if the only moral were to advise children not to let their parents send them to such a school. But Cormier sounds like yet another dispirited radical of the 1968 generation, of Miami and the siege of Chicago [cities where rioting occurred during presidential conventions in the 1960s]. The radical moral taken to heart after a term and a half on the steps of [Richard] Nixon's Pentagon was that *all* structures of authority and institutions were deadly, and all would, in their super-ruthless and efficient way, break the spirit of the individual.

Jerry Renault, the hero in *The Chocolate War*, is first detailed by the bullies to refuse his school duty to sell chocolates for school funds, so that the gang may assert their grip on all pupils by humiliating the deputy principal who has tried to double sales. When the ban is lifted, on his own brave decision he keeps up his refusal to sell the chocolates. The gang, with the connivance of the priests—the collusion of formal and informal Old Corruptions—then beat him up horribly and break his spirit as well as his body. It is at such moments, as is always the case with this familiar genre, that the prose moves with the greatest conviction. It runs its fingernail along the line of the nerve, and the reader wriggles with the routine sympathetic thrill of at once feeling and inflicting pain:

> His stomach caved in as Janza's fist sank into the flesh. He clutched at his stomach protectively and his face absorbed two stunning blows—his left eye felt smashed, the pupil crushed. His body sang with pain.

Hero-victim and reader are left with the pain, and the clichés of concussion. The crude lesson is threefold: that all institutions systematize violence; that violence upholds power without reason; that individuals cannot hope to change these facts. These are the sentimentalities of disenchantment, understandable enough when you are faced with the 'realism' of [U.S. secretary of state Henry] Kissinger's and Nixon's blockade of Vietnam. But they are constantly rebutted in history and they leave no room for the necessary violence without which decency and civilization will not survive.

Inappropriate for a Children's Novel

The Chocolate War is a children's novel. Inasmuch as this is so, the thrill and relish with which it plays on the raw edge of its readers' nerves seem not to spring from the old having-it-both-ways of the realistic thriller as [Richard] Hoggart analyses it. The sex-and-violence thriller—to accept that association—notoriously gained a spurious moral credit by being on the side of right while permitting the reader to enjoy all the sadistic satisfactions of inflicting pain and enjoying cruel power. There may be a touch of this in Cormier's novel, but if the argument I have put about innocence is at all adequate, the more likely responses on the part of a child aged, say,

Some critics of The Chocolate War *say its realism is too raw and brutal for young readers like this one.* Image copyright © Andrey Shadrin, 2009. Used under license from Shutterstock.com.

twelve are horror and incomprehension. Even the toughest egg of the second year expects more justice from life than this, and insofar as the prose is effective in creating the thrill of pain, the novel has something of the realism of a movie like

Marathon Man with its torture scenes in a dentist's chair, or [director John] Boorman's [movie] *Deliverance* with its discomfortingly immediate wounding and dreadful deaths. The writing is never far from the clichés of echo-chamber and beating-up by sound waves, of course, but its vividness makes its strongest effects very hard to negotiate, to know what to do with. The difference in moral climate could be best brought out if one were to compare in tone, reticence, and decorum the description in [Leo Tolstoy's classic novel] *War and Peace* of Pierre's narrow escape from execution after capture at Borodino, and the shockingly unfeeling explicitness with which a crude war novel like [Norman] Mailer's *The Naked and the Dead* details arbitrary murder, mutilation and callousness.

This is more than fixing a fight between the giant Tolstoy and the modern pygmy [i.e., Cormier]. It is also a matter of social convention and literary decorum, particularly since the audience at hand are children. The *intention* of *The Chocolate War* seems to be to force the child directly up against the pain of pain, the facts of cruelty and oppression, by way of showing him that the adults have always told lies about the world's being a fine and benign place, the guardians of the social order being friendly and just, the nature of action being unambiguous and generous. 'Here, kid, this is how it really is.' Time they lost their innocence.

Now adults have often lied, as it is the point of [Mark Twain's] *Huckleberry Finn* to show us. It has already been suggested that some idealizing of what really happens is necessary, not in order to fool children, but in order to show them an image of the finer forms of life. We tell children of a more nearly excellent world not in order to anaesthetize them but as a prompt to the future. Or so the best novelists do. Their business, as it has been the business of this book to urge upon them, is to come to the life they write about with a keen, reciprocal, and animating sense of the finest life they can imagine.

The Chocolate War, and many lesser novels, fails that test. Luxuriating in their radical realism, the authors make an evil of necessity, and leave no means of criticizing on behalf of a better life the oppressions, power systems, and their violences, which the novelists seek to expose. The group of writers in question intend to pull the mask of benignity from society's cruel face, or to show that experience is bitter and painful. . . .

Too Soon for Young Readers

Children, of course, like a dose of the terrors at times—well-controlled times, with a warm fire and all the lights on all the way upstairs to bed. But as we have already noted, the choice to take a deliberate dose probably needs to be nicely balanced against the incredibility of the tale. If ghost or horror stories and films press too hard against the limits of the conventions, then the imaginative experience begins to get out of hand and 'become too real'.

It is not however such studied risk-taking which we are talking about; the author-teachers in hand seek to break the convention, precisely because it doesn't permit them to tell children about the many political menaces and atrocities of the real world, and allows children far too much well-lit room to escape into, on the way to bed or into adolescent life. My objection to *The Chocolate War* and some of its peers is that this determination leads the author-teacher into three related errors all evident in their prose and structure: first, a grossness and indecorum which forces brutal events too abruptly on the reader; second, a raw thrillingness about the prose which makes the authors' attitudes to power very ambiguous—the ambiguity of many modern films like *A Clockwork Orange*; third, the narrative convention which traps us inside the hero's skull and denies us the means of freeing ourselves from and criticizing his plight. The strictures stand; so does the charge that children must know political wrong for what it is.

The Message of *The Chocolate War* Is One of Despair

Rebecca Lukens

Rebecca Lukens taught English literature at Miami University in Oxford, Ohio. She writes extensively in the field of children's literature and is the author of A Critical Handbook of Children's Literature *and* A Critical Handbook of Literature for Young Adults.

In the following selection, Rebecca Lukens compares the changing worldview in the years that separate The Chocolate War *(1974) from J.D. Salinger's* The Catcher in the Rye *(1951). The earlier work, while dealing with depression, still ends on a note of optimism. In contrast, Lukens finds Cormier's vision in* The Chocolate War *to be one of despair and hopelessness.*

Chronicling the quest of Holden Caulfield for people and experience that could verify his most optimistic wishes [in *The Catcher in the Rye*, J.D.] Salinger shows the growing disappointment as Holden finds many of his idols standing upon feet of clay. And yet Salinger's hero, although he writes from a sanitarium, becomes a realist. Many of his idols have fallen, and his quest for perfection has left him with only ten-year-old Phoebe, whose innocence is still inviolate. But Holden will work himself out of his depression; by novel's end he is rising from it. His self-told story shows that within himself are the seeds of good. If there are others like him—and his millions of readers over thirty years prove that to be true—the world cannot be all bad.

Rebecca Lukens, "From Salinger to Cormier: Disillusionment to Despair in Thirty Years," *The ALAN Review*, vol. 9, no. 1, Fall 1981, pp. 38–40, 42. Reproduced by permission.

A World Without Hope

Robert Cormier, on the other hand, begins from quite another premise. The world is rotten; the honest people flee; those who remain are corrupt; the government is ineffectual but controlling; organized violence is ubiquitous. There is no hope. Between 1951 and 1974 the world-view in popular literature flipped; it has gone from realistic *bildungsroman* [coming-of-age novel] showing youth's awakening awareness of evil, as Young Goodman Brown [character from a short story of the same name by Nathaniel Hawthorne] and Redburn [protagonist in Herman Melville's novel *Redburn: His First Voyage*] discovered it, to another world-view: The pervasive forces of the unseen and the sinister are in control. Hope is gone; despair remains. . . .

Brutality opens Cormier's novel, and it crescendoes to unbelievable heights in the final beating. It envelops adult and adolescent; it shows no one with strength sufficient to withstand evil.

The source of the novel's conflict is, or seems to be, Jerry's wish to hold out against The Vigils, to disturb the universe by resisting evil. The real protagonist in the novel, however, is not Jerry but the villain Archie. By skillful use of omniscient point of view, Cormier makes us see Archie's compulsion to keep himself on top. To forestall his own defeat and to retain control of The Vigils and thus of the school, Archie must concoct one more, and one more vicious scheme. Archie must create the terror-producing plans, plans that use his club members for evil, then turn back upon them so that no one can win—save Archie. . . .

In payment for his obstinate refusal to sell chocolates, Jerry suffers. In scrimmage, when he makes his assigned tackle and gets Carter, he suffers a blinding blow to the kidneys. To the macho society of Trinity School, the ultimate disgrace is to be called a fairy, and this Jerry suffers, too. At Archie's charge, Emile enlists the neighborhood children, a ruthless gang of evil tots; wanting to kill him, to blind him, they pile into Jerry, kicking him in the groin. Children, too, are corrupt and ruthless; they join the attack as hired assassins. Archie's Vigils will not suffer disobedience or defiance. They make silent phone calls to Jerry all night long. They call out to him, evening phantoms on the street. They destroy and clean out Jerry's locker so that he does not exist. Ignored by students and faculty alike, he is nothing, no one.

The violence and brutality of the chocolate raffle and the rigged fight conclude the bitter novel. What The Vigils have done to the school and to Jerry, "they would do to the world when they left Trinity." Greed and cruelty—the chance to win a hundred dollars and to see a bloody fight—control everyone. "That's why it works ... because we're all bastards," explains Archie. Finally even Jerry, the last holdout against evil, strikes out furiously and illegally in the ring at Emile in a "beautiful" blow. He is invaded by a "new sickness ... of knowing what he had become, another animal, not disturbing the universe, but damaging it. He had allowed Archie to do this to him."

If *The Chocolate War* had not ended with Jerry's defeat but with the banishment of Brother Leon or The Vigils, or with an uprising that set things at least into a neutral or holding pattern, it would not end in despair. Instead, in the final pages of the novel Jerry wishes he could tell Goober "Don't try to disturb the universe. You can't." Brother Leon, who to serve himself manipulates kids and other priests, remains in power. There is no hope. Despair wins. . . .

The Everyday World Turned Savage

We have always had tales of terror. For generations American adolescents have thrilled and chilled to [Edgar Allan] Poe's gruesome and yet fanciful tales of men and women laughing diabolically at their systems for perpetrating a living death. Poe's characters, however, are mad, insane; readers marvel at

Poe's ingenuity. George Orwell in *1984* creates another tale of terror, this time of a political stranglehold on people's lives. But in the allegorical style of the novel, this is a totalitarian state with language and institutions unlike our own. By using an unemotional narrator who reports happenings in a country different from our own, where an abstraction called Big Brother represents institutional surveillance, Orwell creates distance and objectivity. As for adolescent protagonists, William Golding's *Lord of the Flies* has Ralph who opposes Jack, reason and humanity opposing impulse and violence. Although oblivious to any comment on original sin, readers are struck by their own capacities to relate to both Ralph and Jack and are thus frightened at the potential for savagery they detect in *themselves*. But the fantasy island setting in a remote time permits readers at least to hope that in the here-and-now *they* would not behave with savagery.

Poe, Orwell, and Golding permit us to discover and to contemplate the evil sides of society and ourselves, to search within for the source and the placement of our sympathies, and to hope that we can withstand. Cormier, on the other hand, takes another view. He does not deal with the existential *angst* of humankind—the eternal issue. The immediacy of Cormier's situations, the feeling of "today," the skillfully portrayed reality of the particular evils in the "now," produce terror in the reader. Like Salinger, Cormier disillusions the adolescent reader, but unlike Salinger who offers discovery, Cormier offers only despair.

Social Issues
in Literature

CHAPTER 3

Contemporary
Perspectives on
Peer Pressure

More Laws Are Addressing Cyber-bullying

Ashley Surdin

Ashley Surdin is a Washington Post *staff writer.*

In the following viewpoint, Ashley Surdin reports that the increased incidence of cyber-bullying has led at least thirteen states to pass laws attempting to address Internet-based intimidation. Cyber-bullying is growing, with four in ten teenagers reporting that they have experienced some form of cyber-based harassment. Surdin contends that the issue is made more complex because of the need to balance two concerns: protecting students from harassment and protecting their right to free speech.

In California, a hateful Internet campaign followed sixth-grader Olivia Gardner through three schools. In Vermont, a humiliated Ryan Halligan, 13, took his own life after being encouraged to do so by one of his middle-school peers. And in perhaps the most notorious case, Lori Drew, 49, was recently convicted on misdemeanor charges for posing as a teenage boy on MySpace to woo and then reject 13-year-old Megan Meier of Missouri, who later hanged herself in her closet.

Such are a few of the anguished stories of cyber-bullying that are increasingly cropping up around the country, as more and more children and teenagers wage war with one another on computers and cellphones. The phenomenon has led to a push among states to pass laws aimed at clamping down on the student-spun harassment, intimidation and threats coursing through the Web.

Most of the laws are aimed at school districts, requiring them to develop policies on cyber-bullying—for example, how to train school staff members or discipline students. At least 13 states have passed such laws, including Arkansas, Delaware, Idaho, Iowa, Michigan, Minnesota, Nebraska, New Jersey, Oklahoma, Oregon, South Carolina and Washington. A handful of other states are considering similar measures.

This week, California becomes the latest state to tackle the issue. Starting today, California schools may suspend or expel students who commit cyber-bullying. The law also singles out such harassment as a subject to be addressed by school officials.

"This is part of a trend that is happening across the country, which is basically state legislatures telling the school districts that this is an issue they want them to address," said Nancy Willard, executive director of the Center for Safe and Responsible Internet Use, an Oregon-based organization that provides research and outreach for parents, educators and policymakers on Internet safety. "The message is: Do something."

Though many schools throughout the nation have developed their own policies, some remain unsure how to handle cyber-bullying. It can be time-consuming and difficult to investigate, given the veil of anonymity the Web offers. Educators may not understand the technology that students are using.

But the biggest cause of schools' hesitation, educators and legal experts say, is the fine line between protecting students from harassment and observing their right to free speech. That, Willard said, impels some educators to take a "not my problem" approach to off-campus cyber-bullying.

According to critics of the cyber-bullying laws, that's the right approach.

"The problem with these laws is that schools are now trying to control what students say outside of school. And that's wrong," said Aden Fine, a senior staff lawyer with the national legal department of the American Civil Liberties Union, which

John Halligan shows the Web page devoted to his son Ryan in Underhill, Vermont, on February 7, 2007. Ryan, bullied by classmates for months online, killed himself in 2003. AP Images.

has closely followed such legislation. "What students say outside of school—that's for parents to deal with or other government bodies to deal with.

"We have to keep in mind this is free speech we're talking about."

Willard said it is a mistake for school officials not to pay attention to cyber-bullying outside of school because escalating harassment often spills onto campus. Research also shows that such bullying leads to students failing in school, avoiding class and contemplating suicide, she said.

As it is, schools may discipline students for actions outside of class if they disrupt the educational process, said Kim Croyle, a West Virginia lawyer who represents several school boards and lectures nationally on cyber-bullying. If, for instance, a student calls in a bomb threat from outside school or threatens another student so badly that they avoid school, the school could take action.

The real thrust of the state cyber-bullying laws, Croyle said, is setting a clear expectation for students and educators. "It takes a lot of the guesswork out," she said.

Cyber-bullying occurs when a minor is targeted in some form—threatened, humiliated, harassed—by another, and it is not to be confused with cyber-stalking or cyber-harassment, which involves an adult. Not limited to the Internet, cyber-bullying can spread by cellphones or other digital devices.

Four in 10 teenagers report that they have experienced some form of cyber-bullying, according to a 2006 study commissioned by the National Crime Prevention Council. It is more common among females than males, and most prevalent among 15- and 16-year-olds, according to the study.

Champions and critics of the laws agree that preventive education is a more powerful deterrent to cyber-bullying than discipline. That notion is supported by Patricia Agatston, co-author of "Cyber Bullying: Bullying in the Digital Age" and a counselor at Cobb County School District's Prevention-Intervention Center in Georgia.

"A lot of it can be prevented if we can just teach kids to think before they put things out there," Agatston said.

John Halligan, whose son Ryan took his life in Essex Junction, Vt., after many years of bullying, some online, applauded the national movement to enact cyber-bullying laws. But, he said, laws alone cannot stop the problem.

"I don't think a law would have prevented what happened here, quite frankly," said Halligan, who spends his time telling his son's story to schools.

"Even though what happened to Ryan happened online as well, it really started in school. I think that's the first step that a lot of states are missing."

Programs That Educate Prevent Bullying

Gerri Hirshey

Gerri Hirshey is a reporter for The New York Times. *In the following brief excerpt from her article, Hirshey reports on* Names Can Really Hurt Us *(Names, for short), a program sponsored by the Connecticut Office of the Anti-Defamation League designed to educate students about the consequences of bullying behavior. Based on the premise that most people are bullied because they are different, the program focuses on making potential bullies feel greater empathy toward their victims. Hirshey states that Names is one of a number of programs being developed in response to an increased incidence of school bullying.*

This past November [2006], the Greenwich [Connecticut] High School principal, Alan J. Capasso, greeted an early morning assembly of more than 800 freshmen about to begin a mandatory anti-bias, anti-bullying program called "Names Can Really Hurt Us." He told them, "This is the most important day of your school year." hellip;

Uncovering the Effects of Bullying

Farther north at New Milford High School, Jonathan Henion, a senior, stood before a "Names" assembly of sophomores to share a story he insisted was no big deal, except that it suggested how one small action could make a difference:

"I was standing in the rotunda with friends of mine, about 30 kids. I noticed this small girl walking by. She had on a big backpack filled with heavy books, and she fell. I just stood there watching and thought to myself, 'What a loser.' She just lay there trying to get up. The girl's face kept getting redder and redder listening to the relentless taunting by my friends. Something clicked. I walked over and lifted her up, picked up her books and brushed the dirt off her arms." . . .

Jonathan's little moment was greeted with huge applause; he looked surprised. . . .

"Names," which requires two months of preparation and training by students and staff members, is not a program that any participant or observer can easily forget. There is straight talk. There are tears, hugs, high-fives, laughs, applause and some astonishing apologies. . . .

Over the last 11 years, some 65,600 Connecticut high school students have participated in "Names," which is sponsored and supervised by the Connecticut Office of the Anti-Defamation League [A.D.L.]. Guided by teachers, trained student volunteers and league facilitators, students talk with the unflinching candor of children about topics most adults would prefer to avoid: gossip, rumor, physical harassment, racism, homophobia, depression, eating disorders, self-mutilation, drinking, drugs, suicide—the full range of bullying behavior and its consequences.

Some students who spoke in small group and open-mike discussions are quoted here, but to protect their privacy, neither they nor their schools are identified.

Victims Are Perceived as Different

Marji Lipshez-Shapiro, the Anti-Defamation League's Connecticut regional director of education, who created the program in 1995, said that she first sensed the testimonial power of students' voices when she was dean of residential life at Connecticut College in the mid-1980s. . . .

In group discussions and in an open-mike session, the stories spool out. Often, just speaking them aloud is an act of courage. Witness the overweight girl reciting the names she has been called, the former stutterer who rehearsed for a month to articulate her agonies, the boy rolling up his sleeves to reveal arms crisscrossed with scars from self-inflicted cuts. A popular teacher described the day he heard his gay son sobbing in his room, then found his schoolbooks scrawled with vicious antigay slurs.

On "Names" day, nobody minces words:

"So, um, I've got A.D.H.D., I was finally diagnosed. At least I don't think I'm a freak anymore. I'm on medication now and working really hard. People remember me the way I was, but I'm not like that anymore. I'm not. I'm just asking—give me a second chance, O.K.? Just come up and say, Hi. Please." . . .

In a darkened school auditorium, Ms. Lipshez-Shapiro's eyes welled up when a boy explained how he had to ask his best friends to stop calling him D. J. "Some of them didn't even get it, that D.J. was short for dirty Jew," he said. "They apologized. They really didn't understand how it hurt." It is rare that anti-Semitism comes up in "Names," but Ms. Lipshez-Shapiro explained why an organization devoted to combating that ancient transgression got into the bully business. "At A.D.L., we look at the consequences of being different, at prejudices and stereotyping and discrimination," she said. "The main reason people are bullied is because they're different or perceived to be. Our programs are really anti-bias more than anti-bully. Our goal is to teach empathy to perpetrators. A lot of times they have no idea of the power of what they're doing."

Bullying Is a Growing Problem

Few educators would argue against the need for a positive form of intervention. In 2001, the National Institute of Child Health and Human Development identified school bullying as a growing public health problem. Its commissioned study found that 29 percent of the nearly 16,000 American students surveyed said that they had experienced bullying, either as a target, offender or both.

"Names" is one of many anti-bullying programs being deployed across the nation by concerned PTAs, school boards, community theater groups and even by the Girl Scouts of America. Twenty-nine states, including Connecticut and New Jersey, have enacted legislation against bullying, intimidation or harassment and 11 others are in the process, according to the National Conference of State Legislatures. And New York has passed an education law that requires school districts to devise strategies to deal with violence as part of a school safety plan.

"Wherever we take the program, we've found that the issues raised are basically the same," said a league facilitator, Sandra Vonniessen-Applebee. Though school bullies have been around longer than chalkboards, their playground and their reach have expanded in the information age. Young, media-saturated lives traverse an electronic landscape, peopled with elite "Survivor" and "American Idol" winners and an ever-growing pool of reality show losers. There are bully-centric teenage and kiddie flicks ("Mean Girls," "Ant Bully"). Teenage chick lit series ("Gossip Girl," "The Clique") are bristling with hissy, sarcastic vipers wrapped in Juicy Couture. And there is Bully, a video game that depicts the adolescent atrocities facing the new student in a fictional boarding school.

"It is a pervasive media message that being mean is cool, with put-downs and the like," Ms. Lipshez-Shapiro, said, noting that cyber-bullying, which invokes rumor and insults via the popular social-networking sites Facebook and MySpace, has become a huge concern. . . .

Bullying Education Is Effective

Can bully education work? A pioneering 1988 study done in Norway by Dan Olweus, a social researcher, found that the incidence of bullying in Norwegian schools fell by 50 percent or more in the two years after an anti-bullying campaign; truancy, theft and vandalism also dropped markedly.

George Tejeda, a gang specialist, monitors students departing Los Angeles's Thomas Jefferson High School after more than a hundred black and Latino students were involved in a racially motivated brawl. AP Images.

A follow-up survey of the "Names" program in San Diego in 2000 found that 60 percent of students said that after the session they would be less likely to call someone a name; nearly half reported positive changes in other students' behavior. . . .

. . . The scheduling logistics and expense of a "Names" program can be daunting to already-stretched budgets. The Anti-Defamation League pays $1,000 of an average $5,000 cost, which entails everything from hiring substitutes for participating teachers to audio-visual aids. But school systems across the tristate area are also mindful of a rise in costly bully-related litigation.

In Toms River, a seven-year-old case reached the New Jersey Supreme Court [in] November [2006]. Connecticut, which recently strengthened its anti-bullying law, has seen a spate of suits in Greenwich, Berlin and Stonington. . . .

The Risks Involved

Trying to change the hearts and minds of bullies can be a risky business. Not all schools opt for the open-mike segment of "Names," when audience members line up to speak their minds, though it is very popular with students. League facilitators are at the speakers' elbows, ready to intervene should matters get too emotional. Guidance counselors are on hand for especially fragile speakers.

But in the sessions witnessed by a reporter, it was fellow students, with cheers, group hugs and tissues, who provided the most enveloping and accepting reinforcement. Even those who apologized, among them teary, self-confessed mean girls, were embraced. . . .

"The first year, I got some calls from parents asking, 'What is this race program you're doing?'" recalled Kris Kaczkak, health education chairwoman at New Milford. "But now that parents know what it is, we get great support. Our teachers volunteer anywhere from 6 to 50 hours each of their time. And I have 150 student volunteers for 50 places."

If forgiveness and grace are shining ideals of "Names," both are met in Lorella Praeli, a lively, chestnut-maned senior who delivered a bravura closing address at New Milford's "Names" day.

Afterward, in between accepting hugs and congratulations, she talked about her experiences as a bullying target before "Names" helped her defuse the problems:

"I have a prosthetic right leg; I lost my leg in a car accident when I was 2 1/2. So all my life I've heard rude remarks about it. And I'm from Peru. I moved here about six years ago. So I've faced racism. I've had the words spoken to my face, behind my back and online. You know, PegLeg. Spic. Border Hopper."

Lorella, who has spoken at many other league-sponsored anti-bias events, plans a career in advocacy, perhaps beginning with a law degree. Despite what she has endured, she said she refused to describe herself as a victim, preferring to focus on her conversion from a bystander. . . .

Right after her speech, one student asked her how she expected "Names" to change a whole class, 400 students. Lorella answered: "I told her you don't need to change the whole class. Go for one person first."

Former Bullies Speak Up

Carrie Malcolm, now 24 and a reformed bully, said that "Names" changed the course of her life, though too late for her victim. As a middle school honor student, leader and volunteer, Ms. Malcolm had a secret life as the tormenter, along with six friends, of a quiet girl named Erin. "She was an outcast," Ms. Malcolm said, "and I was the ringleader of making her life miserable.

"I remember chasing Erin down the hallway and into a classroom, singing some awful song that I had made up about her. She was cornered against the blackboard, crying. And I wouldn't stop screaming this song. Then I just walked away and enjoyed the rest of my afternoon."

Hoping to get away from the group, Erin chose to go to a different area high school. In 1997, she was killed in a car accident on the way to class. "We made the last few years of her short life utter hell," said Ms. Malcolm, who, with Ms. Lipshez-Shapiro's encouragement and guidance, told her story on "Names" day as a sophomore at her regional high school in Durham, a year after Erin's death. At Ms. Malcolm's invitation, Erin's mother and grandmother were in the audience. Hers was a powerful, self-lacerating speech. And she says she cannot let the matter rest.

She has chosen a career in public service, tutoring underserved urban students in New Haven as the executive director of the nonprofit Center for Teaching, Learning and Child Development. And she has spoken at more than 25 Anti-Defamation League–sponsored bullying programs for students, teachers and parents. "I really want to get to parents," she said. "My story exemplifies what middle school bullying is like, that nobody really feels they need to do anything about it. Parents seem to ignore it and think it was a regular part of growing up. I stress that it doesn't have to be that way. And I'll do it over and over in front of parents, administrators and teachers, people that have the power to change it."

Another "Names" open-mike session was coming to a close. The final speaker, a rangy boy in a hoodie sweatshirt, had been pacing nervously.

"Ah . . . yo. I just want to say I'm up here talking for me and my friends. You all know us, right? Yeah. I've probably picked on most of you. And if any of us made fun of you, I'm here to tell you we're sorry. It wasn't cool. We're really sorry. Peace."

Bullying Is Often Motivated by Homophobia

Jane Close Conoley

Jane Close Conoley is the dean of the Gevirtz Graduate School of Education at the University of California, Santa Barbara.

According to a recent study, 43 percent of middle school educators, 22 percent of high school educators, and 21 percent of primary school educators report that bullying occurs at their school on a daily or weekly basis. In the following viewpoint, Jane Close Conoley reports that students who are lesbian, gay, bisexual, or transgendered (LGBT), or give the appearance of being so, are at special risk for bullying. She also finds that teachers often fail to intervene when victims of bullying are LGBT. Conoley points out that there are several steps educators can take to deter bullying and to work with victims to help them protect themselves.

Lawrence King (15 years old) was shot twice in his head on February 12, 2008, by a 14-year-old classmate at E.O. Green Junior High School in Oxnard, California. The eighth-grade classmates of the perpetrator and the victim described the "bad blood" that existed between the two because of the victim's openly gay appearance. Classmates admitted that the victim, a child from a foster setting, had been the target of harassment because of his feminine dress, hair arrangements, and other mannerisms that were gender non-normative. Gay-baiting and taunting turned deadly with the announcement that he was brain dead by February 14. . . .

According to . . . [a] recent publication from the National Center for Education Statistics on school safety 43% of middle

Jane Close Conoley, "Sticks and Stones Can Break My Bones and Words Can Really Hurt Me," *School Psychology Review*, vol. 37, no. 2, 2008, pp. 217–20. Reproduced by permission of the National Association of School Psychologists.

school educators report that student bullying occurs at school daily or weekly. Twenty-two percent of high school and 21% of primary school educators report this same frequency. Victims appear to be chosen based on their physical appearance (e.g., weak or obese), clothes, high grades, non-normative looks or behavior (e.g., weird or geeky), and non-normative gender behaviors.

LGBT Youths at Risk for Bullying

Within a social context that enforces behavior standards through threats, taunts, and physical attacks, young people who are lesbian, gay, bisexual, or transgendered (LGBT), or who look like they may be LGBT, or may be questioning their sexual orientation, are at some special risk for bullying with the accompanying threats to their physical, academic, and psychological well-being. . . .

Of some special note is that the social context within and across various friendship groups of young people appear to influence both the frequency of bullying behaviors and the ways in which the bullying is internalized. Further, victimization seems to affect some students' perception of the entire school climate, with victims predictably reporting less favorable climates than nonvictims. Interestingly, as young people progress through school some of their attitudes toward bullying actually become more positive, as they interpret the bullying as teaching others how to behave in their particular organizational contexts. These findings illustrate that both the behaviors associated with bullying and the effects of being bullied on young people are not merely the products of individual histories.

These investigations of system-level forces that operate to promote or mitigate bullying occurrences and effects suggest the need for further inquiry about how the adults in school settings are involved in bullying. . . . [Teachers] are not perceived to intervene or do not intervene, especially when the victims are or are perceived to be LGBT. However, a reality is that some educators may not know how to intervene effectively. They may normalize physical bullying as gender specific to males and relational bullying as specific to females, and therefore part of normal development. Further, adults may believe that children learn to be tough and resilient by dealing with same-age bullies and thus resist intervening as a way to promote self-confidence in victimized children. Finally, and of most concern, some may allow bullying, especially of children from certain minority groups, as a way to satisfy their own aggressive impulses toward those children or groups.

How can adults be educated or recruited to be leaders in creating safe environments for all children? The preparation and socialization of teachers to have both the skills and values to protect all children from bullying depend in part on their teacher education programs and on the norms set within school organizations. University-based programs to some extent do focus teacher candidates' attention on pluralism in the classroom and social justice issues involved with guaranteeing every child equitable access to educational attainment. However, teacher education programs are getting shorter and more prescribed by state regulations toward content standards as pressures to "produce" more teachers escalate. Opportunities to explore a future teacher's values about bullying in general and values toward non-normative sexual behavior or LGBT status in particular are now limited by the pressures to meet increasing state requirements related to content standards. . . .

Teacher education graduates often report back to their university programs that lessons learned at the university are not well supported in the field. Some of these disconnections likely deserve university adjustments, but others illustrate the power of negative organizational norms on novice behavior. For example, if principals and teacher leaders do not demand and model a zero tolerance policy for bullying behaviors, novice teachers may be unlikely to take the lead. Novices that enter organizations that tolerate homophobic humor among the adults may find it difficult to be publicly supportive of LGBT youth. . . .

A Contributing Factor

Bullying motivated by homophobic attitudes appears to be a particular problem within the larger challenge of creating safe schools. Homophobic attitudes are among the last utterable prejudices among adults. With the certitude of religious conviction or state statute as supports, many adults continue to tolerate and participate in denigrations of LGBT individuals. Their behaviors provide negative models for young people and, at least, tacit encouragement to punish non-normative gender behaviors among peers. There is little reason to assume that educators are immune to these negative values and stereotypes unless they have specifically explored their values related to sexual orientation and all children's rights to safe school environments for learning. In fact, given public concern about LGBT adults' access to youth, it is likely that educators may be particularly reluctant to endorse practices that appear to welcome or offer special protection for LGBT students. Such public concern exists despite a lack of evidence that LGBT teachers or students pose any particular sexual or attitudinal risks to heterosexual students.

Teacher educators and school leadership university faculty could (and should) exert influence in this area by arming educators with relevant research findings and with dispositions and values that focus on the needs of all children. . . . Educators must resist the societal error of stereotyping a person by a sexual orientation label. There are many variables that contribute to a child's learning and behavioral tendencies (e.g., education levels of parents, socioeconomic status, qualifications of teacher, temperament). Using sexual orientation to predict anything but sexual behavior is patently imprecise.

University faculty must be courageous to facilitate academic discussions that demand the protection of LGBT youth. Introducing and pursuing these concepts among preservice and in-service educators is likely to invite criticism and, occasionally, censure from various stakeholders (parents, school board members, alumni of universities). Failure to specifically address school bullying and the disproportionate burden of violence borne by LGBT youth, however, is unacceptable.

Strategies to Reduce Bullying

Educators can engage in fairly simple strategies to reduce the frequency of school bullying. For example, they can be present in hallways and staircases during class transitions and on school play yards. Adult monitoring and supervision are powerful deterrents to bullying. Adults can "catch bullying behavior low" to prevent high levels of violence by adopting zero tolerance for name calling, teasing, pushing, shoving, taunting, vandalizing, and so on. Despite the high status enjoyed by many bullies, teachers must sanction negative behaviors and seek administrator and parent support for such sanctioning. Teachers, counselors, and school psychologists can offer victims special training in how to protect themselves through social support networks and can manipulate peer groups to lessen the power of negative norms. Further, teachers can contribute to victims' social status in a variety of ways; for example, by identifying the victim's strengths, positioning the victim with positive peers, and anticipating the victim's success in managing difficult social situations.

A busy teacher or school administrator may rationalize ignoring early warning signs of bullying, but events such as the death of the California eighth-grader described in the opening paragraph can serve as a clarion call that our society is struggling with conflicting forces of intolerance and more open displays of sexual orientations, of declining levels of adult supervision and greater access to deadly weapons. These forces find expression in our schools and demand that adults engage in universal as well as targeted strategies to build environments that enhance the learning and the safety of all children.

The Desire to Fit In Can Be Lifelong

Dolores T. Puterbaugh

Dolores T. Puterbaugh is a psychotherapist in private practice in Largo, Florida.

In the following essay, Dolores T. Puterbaugh contends that many people today mistakenly believe that if they wear the right symbols and think good thoughts, it is the same as doing good deeds. She suggests that peer pressure is at the root of their misplaced zeal and that the adolescent desire to fit in often extends far into adulthood.

In [2008], Veggie Tales (if you listen to Christian radio or have small children, you've got a passing acquaintance with talking cucumbers and zany zucchini) released the film, "The Pirates Who Don't Do Anything." Initially, the protagonists believed that, by dressing and talking like pirates, they were being pirates. They had numerous adventures and close calls in the process of learning that actions, not costumes, describe who and what we are. Too bad it is not fashionable for grownups to go to Veggie Tales movies for their own—and their kids'—enlightenment.

Confusing Impressions with Actions

There is an ancient way of thinking: wear the feathers or fur of some dead predator, eat an enemy's heart, do a dance, and thereby acquire the powers of that predator or enemy. Many people enjoy watching documentaries on television and simultaneously being fascinated and reassured of their own sophis-

Dolores T. Puterbaugh, "Costumes Don't Make the Pirate," *USA Today* (magazine), vol. 137, no. 2758, July 2008, p. 82. Copyright © 2008 Society for the Advancement of Education. Reproduced by permission.

tication by viewing aboriginal people in their traditional behaviors. After all, we never would smear paint on our bodies and jump around in unison, assuming it will trigger supernatural intervention on demand.

In much of the world, religions based on fear and magic have given way to faith based on reverence and reason. The awe-inspiring, "Hear, O Israel! The Lord is our God, the Lord alone," became the foundation for "Do unto others as you would have them do unto you." In all that these two assertions represent, it is doing right things—not just how one thinks or feels—that is intrinsic to the relationship with God and with others. The devolution to assertions such as "the end justifies the means" and "good intentions are the same as an end," required several centuries and a great many very articulate, and very bleak, intellectuals. Elevating the human above the divine did not seem adequate to cheer up the people who were eager to pronounce God dead and mankind free of supernatural fetters. The festering negativity of Karl Marx, Friedrich Nietzsche, Georg Wilhelm Friedrich Hegel, and other thinkers of the late 19th century led to early 20th-century pragmatism: do whatever it takes to reach an objective, which was, in turn, subsumed into progressive politics.

The outcome of these philosophical wanderings includes the bizarre current situation, wherein a great many individuals imagine that thinking the right thoughts and wearing the correct color shirt, pin, or bracelet is the same as doing something useful. The average American is not featured in National Geographic documentaries, but a great many apparently believe they are "making a difference" in some cosmic, consciousness-raising way, by donning a certain color on a specific day.

A woman accosted me one February morning because I was not wearing red. She scolded, "Why aren't you wearing red? Don't you support women's heart health?" Since I already had run 10 miles, eaten fruit and whole grain cereal at breakfast, and participated in worship services, I thought I was being very supportive of, at least, my heart health. I have no control over any other woman's heart health ... but I was not wearing red to raise awareness of how important it is to have a healthy heart. Now, if you are an educable adult in the U.S., you already know you need a healthy heart. If you need me to wear red on a special day to remind you, good luck. The woman who complained about my lack of support for healthy hearts may, or may not, eat right, or exercise regularly, pray, or otherwise support her heart's health—but she wears red on the right day, thereby raising awareness, and that is what counts.

Besides sounding silly, it sounds an awful lot like the group-think of Marxism and the various flavors of fascism. These variations of left-leaning political philosophy assert that the individual is not as important as the group. This mindset spread from extremist movements into less radical forms of modern liberalism. Showing support of the group—whether by exhibiting the Blue Eagle of the National Recovery Administration (see 1930s America) or wearing peace signs—proves you are on the same page. You are on message.

Peer Pressure Beyond Adolescence

Peer pressure apparently is a lifelong dilemma. A great many people are intimidated into wearing the color or ribbon or bracelet of the moment without thinking about the implications. How many staunchly pro-life Christians purchase Susan B. Komen foundation pink pins—unaware that some of that money is funneled to Planned Parenthood? It is easier to put on the pink blindly. This shows you "support" people with breast cancer. It also would be supportive to babysit a cancer patient's kids, pitch in with chores or donate some money for those bills that are piling up. Giving money to a research foundation is generous, but the markedly Pharisaic flaunting of the color-of-the-day seems self-promoting and, simulta-

Peer pressure can still be intense for adults as well as for teens. © Dex Images/Corbis.

neously, demotes the search for treatments for terrible diseases to the emotional equivalent of wearing a jersey with a famous name on it come "Game Day."

There is a stage in life—adolescence—in which the drive to fit in with the group is normal. We only can pray our kids pick a tolerable group with which to identify and separate from us—but separate they will, asserting their individuality by dressing, behaving, and speaking exactly like the other members of their chosen set. We are supposed to outgrow this sometime between about age 15 and early college. The process can get stuck, however. Group-identification and emotions remain primary motives, and the development towards psychological maturity becomes mired.

Nineteen sixties' style liberalism was all about emotions and meanings being paramount. "It's the thought that counts." Well, that is fair up to the age of reason, which, for many religions, is about age seven. After that, outcomes count, too. After all, who buys a kid's story that he "meant" to take out the trash? It either is out at the curb, or it is overflowing in the kitchen and the dog is eating wet paper towels and Styrofoam meat trays. In the personal realm, we very often, and rationally, minimize others' intentions and feelings and meanings. We expect them to step up to the plate with actions.

Thus, we return to the lessons of Veggie Tales—if we do not learn from our vegetables, we may well be mere pirates who fail to do anything.

For Further Discussion

1. In Cormier's interview with Geraldine DeLuca and Roni Natov in Chapter 1, Cormier talks about the opening line of *The Chocolate War*, "They murdered him." He tells how he has to talk to some kids to reassure them that Jerry did not die in the book. What does get murdered in the book?

2. In Chapter 2, Anne Scott MacLeod says *The Chocolate War* is a reversal of the tradition of the American hero persevering against difficult odds and offers a bleak, hopeless vision. Sylvia Patterson Iskander disagrees with her and other critics who see despair and hopelessness in *The Chocolate War*. Iskander suggests that by violating the usual expectations of a happy ending for the hero, Cormier is challenging the reader to take an active role. Thus, Iskander argues, Cormier is telling the reader that individuals can fight for their beliefs. Whom do you agree with, and why?

3. In Chapter 2, Yoshida Junko points out that there are no women in *The Chocolate War*, since Trinity School is an all-boys school and Jerry's mother is dead. Why do you think Cormier has no females in this novel?

4. In Chapter 2, Patty Campbell contends that the reason Jerry refuses to sell chocolates is that he is opposing the forces of evil present in the school. Do you agree or disagree? Why do you think Jerry refuses to sell chocolates?

5. In Chapter 3, Gerri Hirshey reports on the Names program, which is designed to teach antibias, antibullying behaviors. The program is based on the belief that people are bullied because they are different, or perceived to be, and the goal is to teach empathy to the perpetrators. In

The Chocolate War, was Jerry bullied because he was different? Do you think a program like Names would have been effective at Jerry's school? Describe what two of the characters might have said at the microphone.

For Further Reading

Michael Cadnum, *Calling Home*. New York: Puffin, 1993.

Robert Cormier, *After the First Death*. New York: Pantheon, 1979.

——, *Beyond the Chocolate War*. New York: Knopf, 1985.

——, *Fade*. New York: Delacorte, 1988.

——, *I Am the Cheese*. New York: Pantheon, 1974.

——, *We All Fall Down*. New York: Delacorte, 1991.

Chris Crutcher, *Whale Talk*. New York: Greenwillow Books, 2001.

Walter Dean Myers, *Monster*. New York: HarperCollins, 1999.

Robert Newton Peck, *A Day No Pigs Would Die*. New York: Knopf, 1972.

Carol Plum-Ucci, *The Body of Christopher Creed*. San Diego: Harcourt, 2000.

Jerry Spinelli, *Stargirl*. New York: Knopf, 2000.

Paul Zindel, *The Pigman*. New York: Harper & Row, 1968.

Bibliography

Books

Wendy Hart Beckman
Robert Cormier: Banned, Challenged, and Censored. Berkeley Heights, NJ: Enslow, 2008.

Patty Campbell
Robert Cormier: Daring to Disturb the Universe. New York: Delacorte, 2006.

Stan Davis with Julia Davis
Schools Where Everyone Belongs: Practical Strategies for Reducing Bullying. 2nd ed. Champaign, IL: Research Press, 2007.

Robin M. Kowalski, Susan P. Limber, and Patricia W. Agatston
Cyber Bullying: Bullying in the Digital Age. Malden, MA: Wiley-Blackwell, 2008.

Virginia R. Monseau
Teaching the Selected Works of Robert Cormier. Portsmouth, NH: Heinemann, 2007.

Mitzi Myers
"'No Safe Place to Run To': An Interview with Robert Cormier." In *Under Fire: Childhood in the Shadow of War.* Edited by Elizabeth Goodenough and Andrea Immel. Detroit: Wayne State University Press, 2008.

Mitchell J.   *Understanding Peer Influence in*
Prinstein and   *Children and Adolescents*. New York:
Kenneth A.   Guilford, 2008.
Dodge, eds.

Periodicals

Larry K.   "Positive Peer Culture: Antidote to
Brendtro, Martin   'Peer Deviance Training,'" *Reclaiming*
L. Mitchell, and   *Children and Youth*, Winter 2007.
Herman McCall

J.B. Cheaney   "Teen Wars," *World & I*, December
                     2001.

Bruce Clements   "A Second Look: *The Chocolate War*,"
                     Horn Book, April 1979.

William A. Davis   "Tough Tales for Teenagers," *Boston*
                     Globe Magazine, November 16, 1980.

Donald R. Gallo   "Reality and Responsibility: The
                     Continuing Controversy over Robert
                     Cormier's Books for Young Adults,"
                     Voice of Youth Advocates, December
                     1984.

Rachel A. Gordon   "Antisocial Behavior and Young Gang
et al.   Membership," *Criminology*, February
                     2004.

Patricia P. Kelly   "An Interview with Robert Cormier,"
                     Journal of Youth Services in Libraries,
                     vol. 7, 1993.

Robbie
March-Penny

"From Hardback to Paperback: *The Chocolate War* by Robert Cormier," *Children's Literature in Education*, vol. 9, no. 2, 1978.

John McDonald

"Against the Boards: Reflecting on My Youth," *Reclaiming Children and Youth*, Spring 2005.

Nancy
Meyer-Adams and
Bradley T. Conner

"School Violence: Bullying Behaviors and the Psychosocial School Environment in Middle Schools," *Children & Schools*, October 2008.

Perry Nodelman

"Robert Cormier Does a Number," *Children's Literature in Education*, vol. 14, no. 2, 1983.

Richard Peck

"Delivering the Goods," *American Libraries*, October 1974.

Fernanda Santos

"Gang Violence 'Never Happens Here,' but This Time It Did," *New York Times*, April 18, 2008.

Tony Schwartz

"Teen-agers' Laureate," *Newsweek*, July 16, 1979.

Anita Silvey

"An Interview with Robert Cormier," (parts I and II) *Horn Book*, March/April 1985, May/June 1985.

Sharon A.
Stringer

"The Psychological Changes of Adolescence," *ALAN Review*, vol. 22, 1994.

Nancy Veglahn

"The Bland Face of Evil in the Novels of Robert Cormier," *Lion and the Unicorn*," June 1988.

Nancy Willard   "We Hate Ashley," *District
                     Administration*, September 2008.

Index

Cormier's impact on, 36–37,
  54–58
genre of, 18, 38, 61–62
newness of, 60–61
themes of, 112

Youth
  cruelty of, 45–46
  emotions of, 42
See also Teenagers